The Ghost of Tradition

The Ghost of Tradition

Expansive Poetry and Postmodernism

Kevin Walzer

STORY LINE PRESS

1998

Published by Story Line Press
Three Oaks Farm
P. O. Box 1108
Ashland, OR 97520-0052

This publication was made possible thanks in part to the generous
support of the Andrew W. Mellon Foundation, the Charles Schwab
Corporation Foundation and our individual contributors.

Book design by Chiquita Babb

Library of Congress Cataloging-in-Publication Data

Walzer, Kevin, 1968–
    The ghost of tradition : expansive poetry and postmodernism /
Kevin Walzer.
        p.   cm.
    Includes bibliographical references.
    ISBN 1-885266-66-9
    1. Narrative poetry, American—History and criticism. 2. American
poetry—20th century—History and criticism. 3. Teachers' writings.
American—History and criticism. 4. Creative writing—Study and
teaching—United States. 5. Postmodernism (Literature)—United
States. 6. Influence (Literary, artistic, etc.) I. Title.
PS309.N37W35 1998
811'.0309054—dc21   98-39701
                                                              CIP

Contents

Acknowledgements

Though writing is often a solitary process, no book of this sort could be completed without conversation and companionship. For their ideas, suggestions and support, I am grateful to Carole Bonomo Albright, Kevin Bezner, Don Bogen, Michael Bugeja, C.K. Erbes, Dana Gioia, Annie Finch, John Haines, Andrew Hudgins, Robert McDowell, Molly Peacock, Marjorie Roemer, Timothy Steele, Felix Stefanile, and Frederick Turner.

As always, my deepest debt of gratitude goes to my wife, Lori Jareo.

Portions of this book have earlier appeared in the following publications, often in earlier versions:

Chapter I: This essay first appeared in *ELF: Eclectic Literary Forum,* Fall 1997.

Chapter II: One section first appeared in *Sparrow,* October 1995, and was later reprinted in *After New Formalism,* ed. Annie Finch (Brownsville: Story Line P, 1998). Another section first appeared in *ELF: Eclectic Literary Forum,* Winter 1994.

Chapter III: The section on Dana Gioia first appeared in *Italian Americana,* Winter 1998. The section on David Mason first appeared in *ELF: Eclectic Literary Forum,* Summer 1997.

Chapter IV: The section on Molly Peacock first appeared in *ELF: Eclectic Literary Forum,* Spring 1996.

Chapter V: The section on Rachel Hadas first appeared in *ELF: Eclectic Literary Forum,* Summer 1996. The section on Timothy Steele first appeared in *The Tennessee Quarterly,* Winter 1996.

Chapter VII: The section on Jonathan Holden first appeared in *ELF: Eclectic Literary Forum,* Fall 1993.

Preface

The Ghost of Tradition: Expansive Poetry and Postmodernism is the first book-length study of the Expansive poetry movement, devoted to restoring traditional rhyme, meter and narrative to contemporary poetry. The goals of this book are simple: to note the history and growing achievement of the movement; to examine the work of its more significant poets; and to speculate on the movement's influence on contemporary poetry and, more tentatively, literary history.

The time for such a study is due, if not overdue. My basic contention is that the Expansive poets have produced a significant and increasingly influential body of poetry and criticism that bears more serious study—study that they have so far not received in any substantial fashion. It should be clear that my perspective of Expansive poetry, while not uncritical, is sympathetic. My aim is to blend a sympathetic viewpoint with a theoretically informed perspective, to show the way Expansive poetry simultaneously connects with and challenges current issues in poetry, criticism and culture—particularly the complex body of ideas known as Postmodernism. My aim is also to show how Expansive poetry has helped to transform poetry's place in American culture—particularly in its challenge to the creative writing establishment based in universities (a different culture at times antithetical to the literary critical-theoretical establishment, also based in the academy).

Such a perspective has been notably absent from the uneven body of criticism surrounding Expansive poetry. The criticism, what there is of it, can be divided broadly into three categories. The first category is criticism produced by the Expansive poets themselves.

Their essays, while sympathetic and useful for understanding their goals and motivations, are also sometimes limited (like most poetic manifestoes) by the heat of their moment. Such discussion—by poets such as Bruce Bawer, Frederick Feirstein, Annie Finch, Dana Gioia, Mark Jarman, Robert McDowell, Molly Peacock, Timothy Steele, and Frederick Turner—is also generally lacking in specific discussion of poets associated with the movement (beyond short reviews), although many of them have written sensitively about their precursors. (An exception is McDowell's 1996 revision of Harvey Gross's classic study *Sound and Form in Modern Poetry,* which includes discussion of the Expansive poets' return to traditional form and narrative.)

The second category is criticism written by literary critics and theorists who are almost uniformly hostile to the movement, and frequently use the cudgel of literary theory to demonstrate what they contend are its shortcomings. Such academic critics—including Thomas B. Byers, Joseph Conte, and Marjorie Perloff—differ in their emphases, but collectively create a critical environment of unrelenting hostility. Such a reception stands in sharp contrast to Language poetry, a school of poets that emerged simultaneously with the Expansive poets in the 1970s and 1980s. Language poets see language as the source of perception, and write difficult poems that reject lucidity in favor of exploring the varieties of meaning that language creates; their poems are heavily influenced by the mainstream of Postmodern theory, and have been quickly embraced by a theory-driven academy. As Jed Rusala puts it in *The American Poetry Wax Museum,* his wide-ranging cultural history of American poetry since World War II: "When the flagrantly intellectualized, theoretically inflected poetics of the language movement began to surface in academia, it drew the attention not of the house poets but of scholars, critics and theorists" (442). To date, several book-length studies have appeared: *Textual Politics and the Language Poets* (1989) by George Hartley, *Language Poetry: Writing as Rescue* (1992) by Linda Reinfeld, and *The Marginalization of Poetry: Language Writing and Literary History* (1996) by Bob Perelman, one of the inner circle of Language poets.

The third group of critics is poets associated with university creative writing programs. These writers have presided over the explosive growth of the academic poetry subculture since the 1960s; a vast network of creative writing programs, reading circuits, university presses, and writing magazines have comprised the dominant form of poetic culture. These poets also champion an aesthetic that focuses on the depiction of daily human experience, usually autobiographical, in free-verse lyrics. These critics include Ariel Dawson, Wayne Dodd, Ira Sadoff, Diane Wakoski, and David Wojahn. Their essays were usually broad-scale attacks on the Expansive poets for attempting to revive form and narrative; such styles, they argued, were elitist, reactionary and even un-American. The best of these critics was perhaps Jonathan Holden, who argued that the university has fostered an unprecedented health for poetry in American culture and defended his tradition of poetry as the central strand of American poetry over the past three decades. Holden and his colleagues were at times particularly defensive in their discussion of Expansive poetry, possibly because Expansive poetry is a direct rejection of the poetic culture and aesthetic they have created and nurtured.

The Ghost of Tradition aims to fill a void in the critical discussion. The Expansive poets themselves—because of either training or temperament—have been mostly disinclined to link specific poets and poems to the kind of theoretical discussion that is common coin among most literary critics and scholars. (In this respect, they share a weakness with academic creative writers.) Such linkage, of course, comes easily to critical discussion of Language poetry, which at times seems little more than deconstruction with linebreaks. On the other hand, Postmodern theorists who champion Language poetry and avant-garde writing in general refuse even to acknowledge the possibility that contemporary poets could reject the avant-garde (paradoxically the most conservative literary tradition in the late twentieth century) and still reflect current critical concerns with popular culture, the legacies of Modernism, and the relevance of older styles and modes of writing. But these poets call other aspects of Postmodernism—its rejection of individualism and its insistence on the overarching, dehumanizing power of linguistic and historical forces—into question, and Postmodern theorists seem ill-equipped to consider such questions. And finally, academic creative writers, generally viewing Expansive poetry as a threat, cannot offer any kind of useful, disinterested perspective. To them, this is war.

The Ghost of Tradition is divided into seven chapters. The beginning chapters focus on general issues associated with Expansive poetry. Chapter I, "From Movement to Maturity," discusses the Expansive poetry movement's history and characteristic poems, focusing especially on the recent anthologies *Rebel Angels*—the first substantial gathering of the school's work—and *The Reaper Essays*, an important gathering of theoretical justification for the school's narrative wing. Chapter II, "The Ghost of Tradition: Expansive Poetry and Postmodernism," discusses the movement's relationship to Postmodernism. I define Postmodernism as both the current historical period and a larger, theoretical/philosophical body of ideas about Western culture. The chapter analyzes the ways Expansive poetry both connects to Postmodernism and helps to re-define some of Postmodernism's key ideas. This chapter places Expansive poetry in a theoretical context.

Subsequent chapters focus on the work of individual poets. Chapter III, "Still Waters," discusses the narrative lyric sequences and longer poems of Dana Gioia, David Mason, Robert McDowell, and Mary Jo Salter, which delve through quiet surfaces into the darker aspects of human experiences. Chapter IV, "Bold Colors," examines the way four poets explore, in their narratives, extremes of human subject matter—Mark Jarman's California sagas, Marilyn Nelson's family histories, Molly Peacock's wrenching confessions, and Frederick Turner's science-based epics and lyrics. Chapter V, "Strumming the Lyre," discusses the lyric meditations of Emily Grosholz, Rachel Hadas, and Timothy Steele, and the way they use traditional forms to depict contemporary lyric subjects. Chapter VI, "The Sword of Wit," focuses on the ironic, discursive mode of Thomas Disch, Frederick Feirstein, R.S. Gwynn, and Charles Martin, showing how they explore a range of intellectual subjects with wit and nuance.

Finally, Chapter VII, "Expansive Influence: The Exhaustion of University Poetry," suggests some tentative conclusions on the impact of the Expansive poetry movement on poetry's place in the university, especially creative writing programs. The chapter will focus on Jonathan Holden's *The Fate of American Poetry*, which articulates many of the same ideas as the Expansive poets while attacking them. I view Holden's unstated acceptance of many of Expansive poetry's arguments as one measure of its influence. The chapter will also briefly note some of the emerging second generation of Expansive poets.

I should note that these chapters, to a degree, resist the conventional divisions of Expansive poetry into its New Formalist and New Narrative wings—the labels that critics initially applied to these poets in the 1980s, and which are still widely used today. Instead, I use the term "Expansive," first used by Wade Newman in a 1988 essay. The term reflects these poets' interest in expanding both the formal possibilities available to poets, and the audience for poetry in American culture. The term also recognizes the broad affinities between the New Formalist and the New Narrative poets. It is more useful historically, theoretically and aesthetically, to recognize how both strands are related instances of a more general shift in American poetry—a shift the term "Expansive" more fully reflects.

The Expansive poetry movement reminds us of the continuing vitality of rhyme, meter, and story to poetry. Those modes, while not abandoned during the twentieth century in American poetry, were marginalized for much of the time. The main line in American poetry during the twentieth century is free verse and experimentation. While this tradition has produced much distinguished work—Dana Gioia is correct that the Modernist period is the greatest one in American literature—it is also, as we enter not just a new century but a new millennium, a largely exhausted tradition. And yet older traditions have remained, silenced but not quite banished, like ghosts. In the work of the Expansive poets, these traditions have been given bodied form again, and we are reminded of their power to produce beautiful, haunting songs and stories—even (or perhaps especially) in the Postmodern moment. This is the achievement of Expansive poetry. And this is the achievement that *The Ghost of Tradition: Expansive Poetry and Postmodernism* takes as its subject.

The Ghost of Tradition

1

From Movement to Maturity

Today, the Expansive poetry movement has a recognizable definition: to revive traditional rhyme, meter and narrative in contemporary poetry. The critical discussion the school has generated —mostly by poets associated with the movement, and a few hostile critics—has been enough to develop a body of distinctive aims and techniques, and a group of leading poets and representative poems. In short, the movement has assumed a definite shape and influence that gives it a place in American literary history.

Like most literary movements, though, Expansive poetry began not as an organized school but as a number of poets individually dissatisfied with the prevailing modes of poetic style. These poets emerged in the 1980s and devoted themselves to reviving traditional form and narrative, which had, with few exceptions, been marginalized as aesthetic practice in American poetry for much of the twentieth century. These modes were particularly unfashionable during the 1960s and 1970s, when the short, autobiographical, free-verse lyric (owing its influence to the Deep Image, Black Mountain, and Confessional poets) held sway.

The desire of these individual poets was two-fold: to invigorate a mainstream style, lyric free verse, that had grown mannered and orthodox; and to attempt to expand a dwindling, university-based audience by working in modes still relatively popular among a general audience: storytelling (as in films and novels) and rhyme and meter (still flourishing in popular music). In *Can Poetry Matter?,* his influential collection of essays, Dana Gioia articulates some of the concerns that the Expansive poets had:

> At odds with the small but established institutional audience for new poetry, these young writers imagined instead readers who loved literature and the arts but had either rejected or never studied contemporary poetry. This was not the mass audience of television or radio, for whom the written word was not a primary means of information. It was an audience of prose readers—intelligent, educated, and sophisticated individuals who, while no longer reading poetry, enjoyed serious novels, film, drama, jazz, dance, classical music, painting, and the other modern arts. . . . For them, formal and narrative verse did not violate any pre-ordained theoretical taboos, since they unself-consciously enjoyed rhyme, meter, and storytelling as natural elements of the popular arts like rock, musical theater, and motion pictures. (249)

Although solidly established today, the Expansive poets were initially dismissed by many poets and critics who saw their attempt to revive traditional aesthetics as reactionary. These writers preferred free verse, regarding it as the only progressive, aesthetically innovative poetic mode. It is inaccurate to call Expansive poetry reactionary, however, because most of its practitioners also write in free verse—or show an indebtedness to free verse by loosening the traditional forms they adopt. As Gioia notes:

> In my own poetry, I have always worked in both fixed and open forms. Each mode offered possibilities of style, subject, music and development that the other did not suggest, at least in that moment. Likewise, experience in each mode provided an illuminating perspective on the other. Working in free verse helped keep the language of my formal poems varied and contemporary, just as writing in

form helped me keep my free verse more focused and precise. I find it puzzling therefore that so many poets see these modes as opposing aesthetics rather than complementary techniques. (44–45)

A 1988 issue of *Crosscurrents,* edited by Dick Allen, a 1989 anthology of essays, *Expansive Poetry,* edited by Frederick Feirstein, and a 1990 issue of *Verse,* edited by Robert McPhillips, helped to focus critical discussion of the movement. The *Crosscurrents* issue included an essay by Wade Newman, "Crossing the Boundary: The Expansive Movement in American Poetry," which gave the movement its name. Newman identified the movement's simultaneous commitment to "the arts of storytelling . . . and metrical craftsmanship" as its defining features, to expand poetry's audience and range of usable forms (143). In his introduction to the journal, Allen adds another dimension to the idea of Expansive poetry: "Our poetry is Expansive—it moves outward from the Self to reestablish identities with historical, social, religious and scientific realities" (5). Allen also notes that few of the Expansive poets completely reject free verse experimentation: "We try to write free verse so carefully it seems almost formal, just as we try to make our formal verse fit so naturally to the speaking voice it sounds almost free" (5).

Feirstein's anthology went a step further than Allen's by gathering many of the early critical pieces written by the movement's poets into book form, borrowing the name Newman had given the movement. Feirstein's anthology was uneven in its quality, as some essays went beyond polemicism to outright distortion. Feirstein's introduction, written with Frederick Turner, was a particularly bad example of this—going so far as to compare formal poets in the 1970s and early 1980s with writers persecuted in totalitarian countries. "Poets became afraid of writing what was not au courant. After all, for most of them their livelihoods as creative writing teachers depended on it. No university would keep them if they didn't publish. . . . [we] became an odd underground" (xii). Nonetheless, the collection was valuable for the best essays it collected—Gioia's "Notes on the New Formalism," Mark Jarman's "Robinson, Frost, and Jeffers and the New Narrative Poetry," Robert McDowell's "The New Narrative

Poetry," Turner's "The Neural Lyre," and "What's New About the New Formalism" by Robert McPhillips. It is also useful for developing the interconnections between the movement's two strands, form and narrative. Chiefly, the anthology shows the movement in the early process of defining itself.

In his introduction to the 1990 issue of *Verse,* "The New Formalism in American Poetry," McPhillips noted that he first became aware of the term "New Formalism" in 1986. The poets associated with the movement, in McPhillips's view, "expressed the experience of my generation in poetry far more genuinely than either the ideological essays in literary theory that I was studying and trying to emulate in grad school or the programmatic minimalist fictions of either the dirty realists or the urban latenight club-hoppers" (3). Taking the measure of the movement up to that date, McPhillips concluded that it was "a literary movement capable of redirecting the course of American poetry," which "seems likely to remain a vital influence on American poets in the next decade" (3). The issue of *Verse* also contained a mini-anthology of Expansive poems and several essays, including David Mason's "Other Lives: On Shorter Narrative," Gioia's "The Poet in an Age of Prose," McPhillips's "The New Formalism and the Revival of the Love Lyric," and others. At this point, the movement seemed to be consolidating its ideas and beginning to demonstrate its influence. One sign of the initial interest in this new movement was that the special issues of *Verse* and *Crosscurrents* both quickly sold out.

Two recent anthologies show the movement in a different stage of its development: maturity. *The Reaper Essays,* by Mark Jarman and Robert McDowell, gathers—in retrospective fashion—the polemic essays of *The Reaper* magazine, the cornerstone of the narrative wing of the movement, while *Rebel Angels: Twenty-Five Poets of the New Formalism* is a gathering of the movement's poetry. Together, they demonstrate the movement's ascending influence, increasing critical sophistication, and—most importantly—its increasingly fine body of poetry.

The Reaper magazine made its pugnacious debut in 1980, devoted specifically to reviving narrative. As Meg Schoerke notes in her introduction, "*The Reaper* became the only little magazine of the 1980s —even of the century—to focus on narrative poetry and develop a sustained argument in favor of its vitality" (vii). Many of the essays of the book develop this argument in one way or another. From the perspective of the Expansive poetry movement, the most significant essays are "Navigating the Flood," "*The Reaper's* Non-negotiable Demands," and "How to Write Narrative Poetry."

"Navigating the Flood" was the magazine's inaugural essay. In it, Jarman and McDowell argue that "poetry, more than ever, is harnessed by and subordinate to its criticism" (4). This attitude leads to an audience for poetry that "consists only of [critics] and the poets they promote," poets who write poems more intent on formal experiment and showing the poet's cleverness about poetry than story or idea—as if they knew they were writing only for critics. "Are poems extolled by critics like Harold Bloom, Richard Howard, Stanley Plumly, et al., good poems, or merely grist for critical mills? If the latter is true, then they cannot be good poems" (16).

The "non-negotiable demands" include the following:

> 1. Take prosody off the hit list. 2. Stop calling formless writing poetry. 3. Accuracy, at all costs. 4. No emotion without narrative. 5. No more meditating on the meditation. 6. No more poems about poetry. 7. No more irresponsibility of expression. 8. Raze the House of Fashion. 9. Dismantle the Office of Translation. 10. Spring open the Jail of the Self. (34)

These polemical "non-negotiable demands" argue for form as well as narrative, taking on the lax, free-verse, first-person poem so prevalent in the 1970s (and still so today). Jarman and McDowell do "not clamor for a return to the heyday of rhyme and meter, the elegant formal poem, but for a preoccupation with prosody, that will require the new poet to be a master of phrasing, of lines, of stanzas, of form itself" (41).

The primer on "how to write narrative" includes the following traits:

1. A beginning, a middle, and an end. 2. Observation. 3. Compression of time. 4. Containment. 5. Illumination of private gestures. 6. Understatement. 7. Humor. 8. Location. 9. Memorable characters. 10. A compelling subject. (131–133)

These traits identify the typical conventions of realistic narrative, in which the entire story is told, human action remains within the realm of plausibility, and the focus of the story is on character and plot, holding a window up to the world. These are the conventions of most prose fiction of the past two centuries, both the novel and short stories; within fiction, realism functions as the traditional style much as iambic pentameter does in poetry. These conventions have also been largely missing from American poetry since the time of Frost, Jeffers, and Robinson, poets Jarman and McDowell frequently praise.

Not every essay in the book is concerned solely with aesthetic theory, of course. Among the book's other pleasures are a hilarious mock interview with two imaginary poets, and insightful essays on Louis Simpson's work and the influence of Wallace Stevens's meditative poems. Jarman and McDowell view the poetry scene of the 1980s with a cold eye, which makes for stimulating critical thought throughout the book.

Still, from today's perspective, the primary value of *The Reaper Essays* is historical. The book preserves a number of essays that had a measurable impact on the direction of American poetry in the 1980s. The book's historical value also makes some of its polemic bite acceptable in a way that the polemic tone of *Expansive Poetry*— a collection that aspires to historical objectivity even as it takes partisan pot shots—is not.

Unlike earlier anthologies of formal poetry—such as Phillip Dacey and David Jauss's *Strong Measures*—*Rebel Angels* is the first representative anthology of the Expansive poetry movement itself. Its implicit goal is to define a canon of Expansive poets and poems: "We hope to demonstrate that the poets known as the New Formalists have produced poems deserving attention for the beauty, accuracy and memorability of their language, as well as their feeling and ideas" (xv). This the book does. Jarman and David Mason, the editors, provide a brief, useful introduction that outlines the key issues of Expansive poetry, particularly its New Formalist wing. They choose to focus primarily on formal rather than narrative poetry, although they cheat a bit and include such brilliant narrative poems as Gioia's "Counting the Children" and Andrew Hudgins's "Saints and Strangers," both written in a supple blank-verse line. The anthology's major focus, however, is on form.

What makes a prototypical—or perhaps stereotypical—New Formalist poem? Perhaps this question is unfair. But Bruce Bawer's fine poem, "The View from an Airplane at Night, over California," provides a good example:

> This is a sight that Wordsworth never knew,
> whether looking down from mountain, bridge or hill:
> An endless field of lights, white, orange, and blue,
> as small and bright as stars, and nearly still,
> but moving slowly, many miles below,
> in blackness, as stars crawl across the sky,
> and ranked in rows that stars will never know,
> like beads strung on a thousand latticed ties.
> Would even Wordsworth, seeing what I see,
> know that these lights are not well-ordered stars
> that have been here a near-eternity,
> but houses, streetlamps, factories, and cars?
> Or has this slim craft made too high a leap
> above it all, and is the dark too deep? (10)

The first aspect of New Formalism that Bawer's poem displays is, of course, its form: it is a sonnet, of the English variety. But two things distinguish this poem as New Formalist (as opposed to the New Critical formalism so prevalent in the 1950s): its plain language and its depiction of a contemporary urban landscape, a nighttime view of the ground from an airplane. The poem goes further than just depiction of its scene, however; it compares its scene to the urban scenes of London that Wordsworth often depicted in his sonnets. The poem takes measure of how far Western society has advanced since Wordsworth's time. In one sense, society has advanced: humans can fly. But at what cost? A deeper connection to place and landscape, for one. As Bawer asks: "has this slim craft made too high a leap/above it all, and is the dark too deep?" The poem carries on a dialogue with the past of society, and also with literary tradition by discussing Wordsworth's sonnets, among the most important in the genre. This poem, in its way, bears out these generalizations about New Formalism that Jarman and Mason make: "Rejecting the sentimental notion that meter is un-American, New Formalists have contributed to a new consensus, defending the material value of verse against the encroachment of prose, while simultaneously defending popular subjects against the charge of philistinism" (xviii).

Of the 25 poets included in *Rebel Angels,* few are a surprise. The poets featured are Elizabeth Alexander, Julia Alvarez, Bruce Bawer, Rafael Campo, Tom Disch, Frederick Feirstein, Dana Gioia, Emily Grosholz, R.S. Gwynn, Marilyn Hacker, Rachel Hadas, Andrew Hudgins, Paul Lake, Sydney Lea, Brad Leithauser, Phillis Levin, Charles Martin, Marilyn Nelson, Molly Peacock, Wyatt Prunty, Mary Jo Salter, Timothy Steele, Frederick Turner, Rachel Wetzsteon, and Greg Williamson. The most notable omission is that of the editors' work. Jarman's own work, which is narrative, may fall outside the anthology's focus on New Formalism. The omission of Mason's work can probably be attributed to modesty, as his work is formally elegant.

Of course, other inclusions and omissions also invite some disagreement. The inclusion of Marilyn Hacker seems particularly puzzling in this regard. Although Hacker fits generationally, she has long been associated with feminist and lesbian traditions and has never previously been linked to the Expansive poets. Her work has been influential on numerous women poets writing in form—a fact Annie Finch has noted—and perhaps that is why the editors chose to include Hacker. But Hacker, despite her influence, is overrated; her use of form is often stiff, causing strange distortions in syntax, however *virtuosa* it seems. Here is one example from *Rebel Angels*, a sonnet titled "'Did You Love Well What Very Soon You Left?'"

Did you love well what very soon you left?
Come home and take me in your arms and take
away this stomach ache, headache, heartache.
Never so full, I never was bereft
so utterly. The winter evenings drift
dark to the window. Not one word will make
you, where you are, turn in your day, or wake
from your night toward me. The only gift
I got to keep or give is what I've cried,
floodgates let down to mourning for the dead
chances, for the end of being young,
for everyone I loved who really died.
I drank our one year out in brine instead
of honey from the seasons of your tongue. (78)

This poem's rough linebreaks ("make/you," "dead/chances,")
and awkward syntax ("The only gift/I got to keep or give is what
I've cried," "I drank our one year out in brine") indicate the form
mastering the poet, rather than vice versa. Mary Kinzie's observa-
tions of Hacker's technique in *The Judge Is Fury: Dislocation and Form
in Poetry* are accurate:

> Hacker is trying to use stringent stanzaic forms . . . but she has
> thrown off the fetters of the accentual-syllabic line, counting some-
> times stress and sometimes syllables, and sometimes counting both
> ways in the same poem. Lacking any consistent attitude toward the
> line, her rhymes become abstract exercises. . . . This is work that
> practically dares us to find a fault with its skill, and I find little to mit-
> igate my judgment that the gage is thrown by poems in which failed
> irony, dull lists, turgid diction, and a superficial formalism are art-
> lessly exaggerated. (26–27)

Hacker's inclusion clearly seems a gesture toward diversity, made by
a movement nervous about being charged with conservatism—an
accusation its early detractors often leveled. Jarman and Mason con-
firm as much when they praise the poets' "aesthetic common ground
despite their varied social and political background" (xix). Bawer
and Campo, other poets who often include homosexual themes in
their work, are both far more fluid—if less celebrated—formalists.

Toward that end, other poets who might have been included are Kinzie, a gifted formal poet (better than Hacker) and a formidable critic; Michael Bugeja, a prolific poet whose reputation has yet to equal his achievement; and Annie Finch.

Despite these quibbles, *Rebel Angels* is a landmark anthology. It demonstrates the growing achievement and influence of the Expansive poets—a group that has grown past polemic and self-promotion into a group whose work speaks for itself, eloquently. The anthology bears out the assertion its editors make: "These poets represent nothing less than a revolution, a fundamental change, in the art of poetry as it is practiced in this country" (xv). Perhaps a companion volume of narrative verse will one day be needed to fully demonstrate the movement's achievement (as valuable as *The Reaper Essays* is, it is no substitute for the poems themselves—such work as Jarman's *Iris* and *The Black Riviera,* Turner's *The New World,* etc.), but *Rebel Angels* includes enough narrative poetry to suggest the achievement of that side of the movement. The Expansive poetry movement has already produced a substantial body of work—an achievement that *Rebel Angels* clarifies.

It now seems clear that the Expansive poets have progressed from movement to maturity. They have measurably altered the landscape of contemporary American poetry, as the historical focus of *The Reaper Essays* and the work collected in *Rebel Angels* indicate. The initial, polemic work of their movement is done, and the poets are now free to go about their work, secure of respectful (if not always admiring) attention. But they have entered a vastly more difficult phase, because now they are playing for keeps; their movement, and more importantly the poets individually, will be judged by the quality of the poems and criticism they write, and not their relationship to literary fashion. If these anthologies are any indication, however, it is likely that at least some of the mature work of these poets will survive beyond their movement—a surprisingly difficult accomplishment.

2

The Ghost of Tradition

Expansive Poetry and Postmodernism

In the university today, Postmodernist thought colors most discussions of contemporary literature. "Postmodernism," of course, refers to both a historical period—generally regarded as beginning in the 1960s—and a stream of thought, including rejection of universal reason, the dissolution of boundaries between elite and mass culture, and radical political commitments. Given the prevalence of these assumptions, one major question that critics of contemporary literature naturally ask in evaluating that literature is: Is it Postmodern? Texts that receive a "yes" are automatically privileged.

The critical reception of two schools of poetry that emerged in the 1980s is a case in point. The first school, Language poetry, emerges directly from the avant-garde tradition in twentieth-century American poetry; Language poets see language as the source of perception, and therefore experience, and write difficult poems that reject lucidity in favor of exploring the varieties of meaning that language creates. The second school, Expansive poetry, emerges from older traditions of meter, rhyme and narrative; Expansive poets seek to reach a broader audience by infusing their poems with novelistic narrative and traditional forms.

Because of its oppositional stance—characteristic of many Postmodern thinkers—and aesthetic expression of recent literary theories, Language poetry has been privileged by such Postmodern theorists as Frederic Jameson and Marjorie Perloff. In his influential book, *Postmodernism, or, The Cultural Logic of Late Capitalism*, Jameson praises Language poets for seeming "to have adopted schizophrenic fragmentation as their fundamental aesthetic" (28). In contrast, Jameson completely ignores Expansive poetry. Other critics go much further, launching outright denunciations of Expansive poetry as being out of touch with Postmodernist thought, and as politically reactionary for trying to revive older forms such as meter and complex (as opposed to merely anecdotal and episodic) narrative in hopes of reaching the large general audience that still reads novels but leaves poetry aside. Ira Sadoff's charge of Expansive poetry's "dangerous nostalgia" is characteristic: "When they link pseudo-populism . . . to regular meter, they disguise their nostalgia for moral and linguistic certainty, for a universal . . . and univocal way of conserving culture" (7).

The critical milieu that gives rise to such automatic dismissals of literature that explicitly partakes of "tradition" is one thoroughly informed by the experimental, even radical, spirit that followed Modernism into the Postmodern era. Within the field of poetry criticism, the most fully developed expression of this attitude can be seen in Antony Easthope's *Poetry as Discourse*. Easthope focuses on the development of iambic pentameter in English poetry since the Renaissance, linking blank verse with the emergence of the bourgeois, capitalistic society that is the hallmark of modernity. In Easthope's view, blank verse helped to create the very cultural conditions that bring on mass oppression: the tendency of capitalist culture to "naturalize" culture, regarding culture in all aspects as transcendent, unchanging, closed, fixed. Iambic pentameter emerged as an authoritative poetic form during the Renaissance, Easthope notes, and its authority has remained more or less undiminished ever since: "Like linear perspective in graphic art and Western harmony in music, the pentameter may be an epochal form, one co-terminus with bourgeois culture from the Renaissance till now" (53). Easthope argues that iambic pentameter furthers bourgeois culture by creating the illusion of a single poetic speaker, attempting to capture that individual's idiomatic voice by effacing the rhythm of the lines, rather than foregrounding the musical and communal quality of poetry that the older four-stress, oral poetic tradition emphasized: *"it would disclaim the voice speaking the poem in favor of the voice represented in the poem, speaking what it says.* Accordingly pentameter is able to promote representation of someone 'really' speaking" (74; emphasis Easthope's).

Easthope's implication is clear: iambic pentameter is complicit in the unjust, oppressive social structures that capitalist culture creates through its emphasis on individualism and discouragement of collective struggle. His sympathies are evident when he asks, "But if this [capitalist] epoch is over—or if not over, at least since 1848 in its terminal crisis—what happens to the poetic discourse most appropriate to it?" (161). The answer, according to many critics—from Jameson to Perloff—is to reject that poetic discourse. And, in the practice of many poets and the taste of most critics, that is exactly what happened. Easthope champions the Modernist experimentation of Pound and Eliot, which "comprehensively challenges the English poetic tradition, even if it does not succeed in overthrowing it. The whole field of inherited discourse is subverted in one way or another" (134). According to Easthope, to use iambic pentameter today, when bourgeois culture is in unmistakable decline through the efforts of social radicals like Marx and aesthetic radicals like Pound, "is in the strict sense reactionary" (76) because the historical moment that empowered pentameter as a poetic discourse has passed:

> Bourgeois poetic discourse now has no real audience. It is kept alive only in a tainted and complicit form. The state promotes it in secondary and higher education as part of the syllabus for public examinations and 'English' degrees. In Britain the state also subsidizes such poetry through the Arts Council, which gives money for readings and magazines. Meanwhile, people are much more interested in such genuinely contemporary media as cinema, television and popular song in its many varieties. (161)

Easthope's view is sweeping but reductive: he allows no possibility that iambic pentameter, or other traditional poetic form, can be used with any force in the Postmodern era. To even attempt to do so is to, in effect, betray the revolution, to be "in the strict sense reactionary." Discussing Expansive poetry, Thomas B. Byers is less absolutist than Easthope; he understands the danger of establishing the kind of essentialist links between ideology and meter/narrative (401) that Easthope asserts, but he scolds Expansive poetry for being "far from progressive," at odds with what he describes as the mainstream of Postmodern politics: "the preponderance of its utterances range from moderately conservative to virulently reactionary" (398).

Annie Finch, a feminist Expansive poet and critic, argues the opposite case: to her, given the Postmodern emphasis on artifice, on the cultural constructedness of discourse, "the unabashedly stylized use of meter" is perfectly Postmodern. Discussing Easthope at length, she believes that "epochal inappropriateness becomes an unconvincing aesthetic argument against meter" (124). Byers at least allows that possibility; he concedes that meter, rhyme and narrative are not essentially incompatible with Postmodernism:

> Narrative and dramatic, discursive and didactic modes might further undermine the lyric self and implicate the poet in a dialogic play of voices foregrounding history and community. These modes would also help undo the fetishization of the image and the reification of the poem itself. (401–402)

But Byers goes on to charge that

> the movement's laments about how poetry has become too intellectual and inaccessible for the common reader encode a nostalgia for an "ordinary language" theory of poetry, in opposition to the difficulties of both [M]odernism and [P]oststructuralism. . . . It seems that what the Expansivists would like [P]ostmodernism to mean is not that there has been a major paradigm shift in the ways we analyze the self, language and their relationship . . . but that we have, formally speaking, gotten over [M]odernism. (403–404)

Expansive poetry, however, cannot be reduced to a nostalgic, anti-Modernist (or anti-Postmodernist) monolith, seeking to avoid the inevitable pressures of history. Though Jameson ignores Expansive poetry in his discussion of Postmodern aesthetics, a justification for the Postmodernism of Expansive poetry can be constructed from his ideas. Furthermore, certain aspects of Expansive poetry—particularly the essays and poetry of Frederick Turner—call for a redefinition of Postmodernism.

Jameson notes that a major component of Postmodernism is "a weakening of historicity, both in our relationship to public History and in the new forms of our private temporality" (6)—the loss of a sense of historical continuity and unity, replaced with the sense of a constant present. Aesthetically, this leads to "the random cannibalization of all styles of the past, the play of random stylistic allusion, and in general what Henri Lefebvre has called the increasing primacy of the 'neo'" (18). Stylistic expressions, or images, of the past are all that we have left to evoke a historical sense, in this view; nostalgia films, for instance, approach "the 'past' through stylistic connotation, conveying 'pastness' by the glossy qualities of the image, and '1930s-ness' or '1950s-ness' by the attributes of fashion" (19).

Expansive poetry does not self-consciously conform to a theoretical Postmodernist paradigm. But Dana Gioia's description of the practical strategies Expansive poets use to recapture a broader audience show the movement to be consistent with the Postmodernist moment:

> Having found high culture in shambles, the New Formalists looked to popular culture for perspective. In film, rock music, science fiction, and the other popular arts, they found the traditional forms and genres, which the academy had discredited for ideological reasons, still being actively used. Innocent of theory, the general public had somehow failed to appreciate that rhyme and meter, genre and narrative were elitist modes of discourse designed to subjugate their individuality. . . . What the New Formalists—and their counterparts in music, art, sculpture, and theater—imagined was a new imaginative mode that took the materials of popular art—the accessible genres,

> the genuinely emotional subject matter, the irreverent humor, the
> narrative vitality, and the linguistic authenticity—and combined it
> with the precision, compression, and ambition of high art. (253)

Expansive poets make use of a number of elements of popular cul-
ture in their work. Turner writes epic science fiction poetry, *The
New World* and *Genesis*. Vikram Seth's *The Golden Gate* is a novel-
in-verse about Silicon Valley yuppies. Robert McDowell retells the
Lindbergh kidnapping case in *Quiet Money*. In *Take Heart*, Molly
Peacock often explores feminist themes in daily life. Gioia has pub-
lished dramatic monologues in the voices of characters from John
Cheever and Raymond Chandler's fiction.

As this brief catalogue shows, Expansive poetry is a manifesta-
tion of poetic Postmodernism described by Jameson—though Gioia
would likely not describe Expansive poetry as "the random canni-
balization of all the styles of the past." But the increased range of
poetic modes of discourse that Expansive poetry makes possible
demonstrates its consistency with Postmodernism. That increased
range—which partakes of popular culture—also points to the great-
est historical context that Expansive poetry rebels against: poetic
Modernism. Certain critics, like Jonathan Holden in *The Fate of
American Poetry*, dismiss Expansive poetry not on ideological grounds
but on the belief that the movement does nothing new poetically.
Holden sees Expansive poetry as one that "retrieved the strand of
ironic, fixed-form, 'late-[M]odernist' poetry, which had reigned
briefly in the late fifties, a strand epitomized, perhaps, by the vintage
work of Richard Wilbur" (37). But Gioia takes pains to note the dif-
ferent cultural assumptions of the two groups of formalists. Poets
of the older generation, whose consciousness was formed by World
War II, "saw themselves as guardians of the imperiled traditions of
European high culture . . . they wrote poems that displayed their full
command of the traditions of English literature, informed and en-
ergized by international Modernism" (250–252); this was the poetry
that the New Criticism was designed to explicate. In contrast, Ex-
pansive poets—largely comprised of baby boomers, the same gen-

eration whose literary critics contributed heavily to the replacement of New Criticism with the various ideological approaches that so dominate critical discourse—came of age during the Vietnam era and the dissolution of cultural certainty that Gioia alluded to earlier; the different, Postmodern culture they faced as writers led them to imagine their poetic audience, and to shape their poems, differently.

The fact that Expansive poets can use traditional forms like meter and modes like narrative and satire in such a way that they do not immediately evoke the weight of the entire Western tradition in poetry contradicts a central assumption of Byers's argument: that while there is no essential link between meter and ideological conservatism, the historical link between them is so strong that it might as well be essential. While Gioia and Jameson use different language, they are describing the same phenomenon: the recuperation of traditional aesthetics from past historical contexts. This application of traditional aesthetics to Postmodern use can be seen in a variety of Expansive poems.

"In Chandler Country," one of Gioia's poems from his collection *Daily Horoscope,* is one example of Expansive poetry's Postmodernism:

> California night. The Devil's wind,
> the Santa Ana, blows in from the east,
> raging through the canyon like a drunk
> screaming in a bar.
>   The air tastes like
> a stubbed-out cigarette. But why complain?
> The weather's fine as long as you don't breathe.
> Just lean back on the sweat-stained furniture,
> lights turned out, windows shut against the storm,
> and count your blessings.
>   Another sleepless night,
> when every wrinkle in the bedsheet scratches
> like a dry razor on a sunburned cheek,
> when even ten-year whiskey tastes like sand,
> and quiet women in the kitchen run

their fingers on the edges of a knife
and eye their husbands' necks. I wish them luck.

Tonight it seems that if I took the coins
out of my pocket and tossed them in the air
they'd stay a moment glistening like a net
slowly falling through dark water.
                              I remember
the headlights of the cars parked on the beach,
the narrow beams dissolving on the dark
surface of the lake, voices arguing
about the forms, the crackling radio,
the sheeted body lying on the sand,
the trawling net still damp beside it. No,
she wasn't beautiful—but at that age
when youth itself becomes a kind of beauty—
"Taking good care of your client, Marlowe?"

Relentlessly the wind blows on. Next door
catching a scent, the dogs begin to howl.
Lean, furious, raw-eyed from the storm,
packs of coyotes come down from the hills
where there is nothing left to hunt. (7–8)

This poem is specifically Postmodern in the way it adapts a tradi-
tional form—the blank-verse dramatic monologue speaker—and
appropriates a pop-cultural icon. The speaker of the poem is Phillip
Marlowe, the hard-boiled Los Angeles detective from Raymond
Chandler's fiction. Gioia evokes both the stoic weariness of the de-
tective—sleeping in his office on sweat-stained furniture, breathing
smoggy air—and the haggard beauty of a dusty, stormy Southern
California night, recalling the atmosphere of Chandler's fiction. But
this is poetry; despite its casual language, appropriate for its charac-
ter, the poem is written in a subtle iambic pentameter very different
from that of Wilbur or James Merrill. Gioia's use of Marlowe's per-
sona reflects, as Jameson says of Postmodernism in general, a fasci-
nation "precisely by this whole 'degraded' landscape of schlock and
kitsch, of TV series and Reader's Digest culture, of advertising and

motels, of the late show and grade-B Hollywood film, of so-called paraliterature, with its airport paperback categories of the gothic and the romance, the popular biography, the murder mystery, and the science fiction or fantasy novel: materials they no longer simply 'quote,' as a Joyce or a Mahler might have done, but incorporate into their very substance" (2-3). Gioia adopts the persona of Marlowe for several purposes: to evoke a particular mood about California through a familiar character, given the poem's placement in a group of poems about Gioia's childhood in California; to attract readers of fiction to poetry by animating a well-known author's work in verse; and to experiment formally. Robert McPhillips notes this aspect of the poem when he observes, "Gioia experiments with the shape of a poem written in particularly intense blank verse. In so playing with the lines of the poem, Gioia can simulate the looser lines of the hard-boiled prose that is the source of the poem's language, even as, by elevating the prose to the level of blank verse, he can comment on the poetic element in Raymond Chandler's fiction" (323). Clearly, the poem is not at odds with the Postmodernist moment.

Another poem, "Say You Love Me" from Molly Peacock's collection *Take Heart*, is a different example of Expansive poetry's Postmodernism. Written in terza rima, the poem narrates an incident with an abusive, alcoholic father. The drunken father hovers over the poem's speaker, his fifteen-year-old daughter, demanding she declare her affection for him:

> What happened earlier I'm not sure of.
> Of course he was drunk, but often he was.
> His face looked like a ham on a hook above
>
> me—I was pinned to the chair because
> he'd hunkered over me with arms like jaws
> pried open by the chair arms. "Do you love
>
> me?" he began to sob. "Say you love me!"
> I held out. I was probably fifteen. (9)

The speaker tries to resist her father's demands, but they begin to wear her down. "'DO YOU' was beginning to peel, as of live layers of skin" (9). His pathetic, drunken sobs overpower her anger: "my game/was breaking down because I couldn't do//anything, not escape into my own/refusal, *I won't, I won't,* not fantasize/a kind, rich father" (10). She gives in:

> unknown to me, a voice rose and leveled
> off, "I love you," I said. *"Say, 'I love you,*
> *Dad!'"* "I love you, Dad," I whispered, leveled
>
> by defeat into a cardboard image, untrue,
> unbending. (10)

At this point, the speaker tries to get up and leave the room, but her father still looms over the chair. She must depend on the intervention of her sister, who yells to her father that the phone is ringing. Although it is not ringing, he is too drunk to notice immediately and moves toward it, giving the narrator a chance to run. But though she is out of his shadow, there is still no chance for escape:

> He had a fit—
> "It's not ringing!"—but I was at the edge of it
> as he collapsed into the chair and blamed
>
> both of us at a distance. No, the phone
> was not ringing. There was no world out there,
> so there we remained, completely alone. (10)

This poem is Postmodern in the way it uses terza rima to express a strikingly feminist content. In an irregularly rhymed stanza, a young woman confronts oppression directly—an extorted declaration of love. The terza rima form is especially suitable for narrative poetry, as the rhyme and short stanzas (frequently enjambed in Peacock's use of the form) propel the poem forward—recalling Dante, who invented the form for his epic journey poem. Each stanza reveals a small part of the scene, always ending without punctuation, driving the emotional battle between the speaker and her father: "my game/was breaking down because I couldn't do/anything,/. . . . I was at the edge of it/as he collapsed into the chair and blamed/both of us at a distance" (10).

In the first example, the stanza break emphasizes the speaker's helplessness by placing "anything" in isolation; in the second example, the stanza break reinforces the speaker's alienation from her father, as blame is made over the literal distance from one stanza to the next. The breaks in stanzas, unfolding each part of the scene in isolation, are balanced by Peacock's use of rhyme, although many of them vary the standard terza rima scheme (the last three stanzas rhyme *aba bba cdc,* for instance); rhyme in this context serves to join the scene depicted, knitting a young woman's battle against patriarchy's power into a single whole. By establishing a structural tension between stasis and progress, the terza rima is not only useful but the most appropriate form for the feminist conflict depicted in the poem.

The flowering of the feminist poetry movement in America, ably described by Alicia Ostriker in *Stealing the Language,* is clearly part of the emergence of the more Postmodern historical consciousness in American culture. To be sure, most poetry emerging from that movement has tended toward open form. In her introduction to *A Formal Feeling Comes: Poems in Form by Contemporary Women,* Finch acknowledges this point: "For serious twentieth-century women poets, traditional poetic form has had a troubled legacy" (1). But as Peacock's poem shows, contemporary women poets, with the history of Modernist experimentation and feminist advances behind them, are finding genuinely contemporary, Postmodern uses for tradition. Finch argues:

> At their best, these poets combine the intellectual strength, emotional freedom, and self-knowledge women have gained during the twentieth century with the poetic discipline and technique that have long been the female poet's province. These poems point the way to a true linking of the strengths of the old with the strengths of the new: not a nostalgic return to the old forms but an unprecedented relationship with their infinite challenges. (5–6)

Gioia echoes these ideas in another essay, "Notes on the New Formalism," in which he addresses the broad concept of Postmodernism, which he calls "an attractive term the meaning of which no two writers can agree on precisely because it does not yet have one" (39). But he draws connections between the emergence of Expansive poetry and the Postmodern re-invigoration of modernity's other "epochal forms" (to use Easthope's term)—the "return to tonality in serious music, to representation in painting, to decorative detail and nonfunctional design in architecture" (39). He believes that "these revivals of traditional technique (whether linked or not to traditional aesthetics) both reject the specialization and intellectualization of the arts in the academy over the past forty years and affirm the need for a broader popular audience" (40). Gioia sees art as a distinct form of discourse engaging people on matters of fundamental human concern in a way no other mode of discourse can; though this view is a traditional one that Modernism did not abandon, it has taken a pounding in Postmodernist theory which insists on equating art with ideology, and Gioia's implicit hope that the older viewpoint can be restored to respectability. And why not? When Byers dismisses Expansive poetry for being out of touch with Postmodernism, he is, in effect, saying that it does not adhere to progressive ideology. But Postmodernism is a cultural-historical concept as well as a set of ideological assumptions; if it encompasses all of contemporary culture as Jameson suggests it does, then it encompasses all political persuasions, including the center (where most Expansive poets, who argue for the separation of aesthetics and partisan politics, could be situated) and even the right.

In one sense, it is easy to understand why many Postmodernist critics view Expansive poetry as simply a reaction against Postmodernism; one of their key assumptions, that the Western tradition must be deconstructed, cannot lead them to see another conclusion. Even Jameson regards the Postmodern use of tradition as the ransacking of tombs. But even though Expansive poetry is Postmodern, it contains an implicit critique of mainstream Postmodern thought, which is almost invariably leftist. First, and most obvious, Expansive poets believe that Postmodernism must include a recognition that traditions are living, not dead. Turner makes the most forceful argument about this point; he believes that traditional aesthetics such as poetic meter and musical tonality are part of a fundamental human nature that emerged as human culture and biology evolved together. He argues that a true synthesis of fundamental human traditions and contemporary culture are necessary for human society to move forward: "In this work ancient wisdom and traditional lore will join hands with the most sophisticated study of genetics, paleoanthropology, cognitive science, cultural anthropology, ethology, sociobiology, the oral tradition, and performance theory. The word that describes our historical experience of the joining of old and new is Renaissance" (*Tempest, Flute and Oz* 32). Turner is one of a group of thinkers who regard themselves as Postmodern, but distinguish themselves from the Postmodernist mainstream; David Griffin terms this group "constructive" Postmodernists, as opposed to the "deconstructive" mainstream, because they regard deconstructive thought as ultimately paralyzing (20). Turner calls this political position "the radical center."

Expansive poetry critiques deconstructive Postmodernism in another way: the sincerity of its commitment to mass culture. Despite the industriousness of scholars and theorists who discuss mass culture, their scholarship is seldom addressed at those who actually live in such culture. As Gioia perceptively notes, "While many influential literary theorists passionately discuss popular culture in general terms, they rarely show much enthusiasm about its gaudy particulars. Since their interest is primarily ideological, politics not pleasure becomes their governing principle. Unlike the actual audience for popular art, they view it in generically abstract terms—often with an unconscious element of professorial condescension" (254). In fact, Expansive poetry emerged in direct reaction against the entire academic culture that has been poetry's sole patron for half a century. Expansive poetry aims to reach a general audience, using the materials of mass culture. Of course, it goes without saying that poetry, Expansive or not, will not have as large an audience as Rosanne Arnold or Michael Jackson; not even Joyce Carol Oates, a novelist as popular as she is good, has that many readers, which would comprise a genuinely mass audience. But it may be possible for poets to reach an audience of the substantial size that Oates does command. And it seems logical that accessible, but still good, poetry has a greater chance of doing so than Language poetry, which actively rejects accessibility. Even though Language poetry also emerged outside the university, and thrives with a small audience of poets and followers of the avant-garde, it commands no substantial audience in the general culture—for all of its progressive, even radical, aims. Unless populism no longer suggests democracy, Expansive poetry cannot be faulted on ideological grounds.

As Gioia notes, "the dialectic of history is still moving too fast" to render final judgments about Postmodernism (39). Turner views mainstream, deconstructive Postmodernism as "an uneasy phase of transition" to the future world he envisions (*Tempest, Flute and Oz* 3). Even if Turner is ultimately wrong, however, it is clear that mainstream Postmodern discourse is incomplete; even Byers acknowledges that "the politics of Postmodern theory are as complicated as the politics of poetic form" (404), and there must be room in Postmodernism for discourse other than the deconstructive variety— particularly because the dominant mode cannot recognize a serious, genuine approach to poetic art and poetic audience that lies outside its assumptions. Those assumptions even influence the direction of Postmodern poets (such as the Language poets) who claim to repudiate Modernism, but instead represent its decadent late phase (in the sense that late Victorian writing represented the decadent end of Romanticism as a period style in nineteenth-century England). Because the Expansive critique of Modernist and Postmodernist thought is a sophisticated one, it is worth considering some of its main arguments individually, in more depth.

One of the central aspects of the Expansive movement is a reconsideration of the legacies of Modernist poetry in the twentieth century. The central questions: What historical factors led to lyric free verse becoming the dominant mode in American poetry since the second decade of this century, and why were other modes devalued? How has this fact affected our understanding of American poetic history, particularly of earlier periods? And what directions does this fact forecast for the future? The dominance of lyric free verse is a direct result of high Modernism's enormous and continuing influence on American poetry—the seminal ideas and poems of Eliot, H.D., Moore, Pound, Stevens, Williams, and their successors. The experiments of that period were varied, but share a common denominator: presentation of direct objects and experience, in free verse, without interpretation, in short units (whether individual poems or fragments of a larger whole, as in Pound's *Cantos*). Narrative in its traditional sense was largely abandoned, as were most of the traditional meters and forms of English-language verse (in spite of the brief revival of such forms in the elaborate New Critical poems of the 1940s and 1950s). Modernism, in fact, represents one of the most sweeping aesthetic revolutions in English-language poetry of any period.

Like any successful revolutionaries, however, the Modernists and their successors changed more than the present system; they changed our sense of the past. Traditional form and narrative were not just set aside in the present, they were devalued—if not erased—in earlier periods. As Gioia has pointed out, the popular tradition of formal, narrative nineteenth-century poetry—exemplified by Longfellow, Whittier, Sigourney, and others—has, since the Modernist period, been downplayed in favor of Emerson, Whitman, and Dickinson. If poets such as Longfellow are studied, it is as historical figures only, and not for their relevance for contemporary poetry. Modernist assumptions about poetry have colored our sense of poetic history, foregrounding those traditions that connect to the narrow Modernist aesthetic, and relegating others to the margins.

This last point, about Modernism's coloring of poetic history, is the consensus emerging in such books as Timothy Steele's *Missing Measures: Modern Poetry and the Revolt Against Meter* (1990) and Annie Finch's *The Ghost of Meter: Culture and Prosody in American Free Verse* (1993) and *A Formal Feeling Comes: Poems in Form by Contemporary Women* (1994). Steele examines Modernism itself in depth, demonstrating the flaws and unintended consequence of Modernist theorizing about poetic form—its failure to develop a new sense of measure to replace the old rhyme/meter system, a consequence magnified by Modernism's enormous influence. Finch examines two issues: how Modernist free verse never quite escaped meter, and the implications of Modernism for feminism and the long-running tradition of formal poetry by women.

In *Missing Measures,* Steele devotes considerable effort to critiquing Modernism and its aftermath. The book is a comprehensive analysis of the Modernist free verse revolution, examining in meticulous detail the assumptions of the Modernist poets—particularly Eliot, Pound and Williams—in their experimentation with free verse, and the unintended consequences of that experimentation.

Steele suggests that the key assumption of the Modernists—an erroneous one, he argues—is their identification of the stilted formalism of late Victorian poetry with meter itself, and their conclusion that to renovate poetry required abandoning meter. This is a radical step compared to the earlier innovators that T.S. Eliot often compared the Modernists to; the Romantic and, before them, Augustan poets altered poetry's subject matter and diction but did not reject meter itself. "[The Modernists] believed that in order to get rid of Victorian style they also had to get rid of meter, which of course had been employed by the Victorians but was not specifically Victorian, having been used by centuries of earlier poets" (6–7).

The Modernists rejected meter for several reasons, Steele suggests. One reason is related to the Modernists' cultural anxiety over the status of verse, which by the nineteenth century had lost its status as the primary literary art to prose, a significant shift. He notes: "Much of the history of prose style concerns efforts to make prose as memorable and as attractive as verse and to secure for prose a quasi-metrical integrity so that it can achieve an emotional power comparable to poetry" (9). The Modernists took the opposite view: "Whereas in earlier times prose writers experimented with incorporating verse cadences into prose, poets now began to experiment with integrating the relative rhythms of prose into verse. Prose becomes, in short, the primary art. In this context, Ford Madox Ford and Ezra Pound's assertion that, as Ford puts it, 'verse must be at least as well written as prose if it is to be poetry,' gets transmuted into the notion that verse might profitably be written as the novel is written—without meter" (9).

The reason the Modernists felt they could write poetry without meter descends from an ancient philosophical confusion over the definition of poetry. Steele identifies a conflation by Renaissance philosophers of Aristotle's *Poetics* with Quintilian's *Institutes of Oratory*, which drew a distinction between poetry (in the Renaissance, writing that especially and intensely imitates nature) and verse (writing in meter). Though the contexts of this distinction changed over the centuries, the distinction itself remained, and the Modernists frequently made use of it in their essays. In Modernist theory and practice, Steele notes, the idea "that poetry is something *more* than meter is transformed into the idea that poetry is something *other* than meter. One finds in much Modern criticism, especially in that of Eliot, the belief that conventional metrical composition is less admirable than poetry which eschews regular meter in preference for some more 'difficult' quality of rhythm" (10).

Another factor in the Modernists' sense of poetic purity is nineteenth-century aestheticism, its emphasis on formal purity, and its notions of organic form. Aestheticism—the "art for art's sake" movement with roots in Kant's *Critique of Judgment*—treated works of art as autonomous, unified creations, whose qualities were judged only through a response to the work itself, and not by extrinsic standards. Steele notes, "If every poem is defined in terms of an independent internal unity, it follows that every poem may or even should create its own prosody" rather than follow a fixed, predetermined form (11). Accompanying an artistic emphasis on purity is an elevation of music —the most purely formal, non-referential form of art—to the top of artistic hierarchy, reflected in Pound's command that poets should "compose in the sequence of the musical phrase, not in sequence of a metronome." This command focuses on the broad category rather than the more narrow category of fixed metrical measure, and not only allows free verse, but privileges it as the more "pure" formal practice (12).

Buttressing this elevation of free verse's formal purity over traditional form is a shift in poets' understanding of the phrase "organic form," a term that parallels aesthetic practice with the natural world. In the Romantic period, poets saw no contradiction between nature and meter since, in their view, nature proceeded according to fixed principles of development. By the turn of the century, though, poets' definition of "organic form" had changed:

> Rather than urging that poets should create, as nature does, according to certain regulating principles of development, some observers contend that poets should function, as nature functions, unconsciously. And rather than imitating the comeliness of natural objects, some poets, such as D.H. Lawrence, seek to suggest the internal processes that determine those objects. To the extent that these processes are regarded as being elementally turbulent or chaotic, verse that is intentionally confused comes to be considered truer to nature than is verse of a more orderly kind. To the extent that metrical speech embodies clear structural principles, it is therefore discouraged as not only unnecessary to poetical-natural truth but inappropriate to it. (12)

This shift in definition of organic form parallels scientific developments in the nineteenth and early twentieth centuries—particularly those of Darwin, Freud, and Einstein—and leads to what Steele identifies as the final factor in the free-verse revolution, the influence of science on poets.

Scientific discourse exerted great influence on the Modernist poets. Although they were in certain senses deeply rooted in tradition —the range of reference in *The Waste Land* and *The Cantos,* as well as Eliot's essay "Tradition and the Individual Talent," proves this point —the Modernist poets also saw themselves as innovators in the same sense as Darwin, Freud, and others, innovators whose ideas radically changed the world in which they lived. In their view, relentless experimentation—constantly introducing new ideas and forms that would subsume earlier ones, or render them obsolete—was the only way to write genuine poetry in the Modern world: "The modern's leaders transferred to poetry this model of scientific history.

This transferral undermined the older view that, in poetic composition, the safest guides are provided by the examples of earlier masterpieces. In addition, the transferral encouraged the notion that the literary past is, like the scientific past, largely irrelevant to present practice" (14).

Steele's response to this conclusion is one of frank despair. He is worth quoting at length:

> What happened was different from what the leaders of the Modern movement anticipated. Their revolution triumphed. But a new metric did not emerge. And the inheritors of the legacy of the Modern movement, their numbers growing from decade to decade, simply went on writing without meter. The interim period was repeatedly and indefinitely extended. Originally a means of examining the old measures or of testing whether new measures were possible, free verse itself became a "form." Whereas the early experimentalists had pursued heterodox versification in the interests of poetic purity, their followers employed such procedures in an increasingly casual fashion, the revolution having undermined the metrical tradition and metrical awareness that gave the procedures significance in the first place.
>
> . . . .
>
> Today, one almost hesitates to say that most poets write unmetrically: such a statement suggests that they know what meter is, which does not appear to be the case. Rather, it seems that versification, as it has been understood for millennia, is for the majority of contemporary poets an irrelevant matter. And looking back across our century, one may feel that metrical tradition resembles a signal which has been growing fainter and fainter. (280–281)

Taken as a factual description of twentieth-century poetic practice, Steele's conclusion is indisputable. Free verse is the *lingua franca* of twentieth-century American poetry, the dominant form. Although Steele cites brief revivals of traditional form in the 1950s, and distinguished work in traditional forms by individual poets throughout the century, these exceptions prove the rule of free verse.

If free verse is the rule, Finch suggests that the best free verse necessarily emerges from an engagement with metrical tradition. In

The Ghost of Meter, Finch argues that free verse does not escape metrical traditions very easily. In fact, Finch suggests, poets writing in free verse often confront the traditions of meter directly, with metrical patterns creeping in and out of their work in revealing ways. She terms this relationship between poetic meter—however covert, even unconscious—and poetic meaning "the metrical code." Finch argues that meter

> can constitute a crucial aspect of the meaning of poems written during times of metrical crisis—periods of deep change in the prosodic foundations of poetry. The words in such poems comment, on one level, on their own meter, just as meter enriches the meaning of the words. Metered lines of metrically variable verse can reveal the poet's attitudes toward the meter's cultural and literary connotations. (1)

Finch demonstrates the validity of this theory in readings of Dickinson, Whitman, Stephen Crane, and Eliot. Her chapters on Dickinson and Eliot are particularly illuminating. As a female poet in the nineteenth century, Dickinson faced enormous obstacles in establishing poetic authority; most male writers simply did not take female writers seriously. Thus, female writers, to establish their own voices as writers, had to conform to literary convention while subverting it; Dickinson did so by writing mostly in hymn or ballad meters. Finch points out that Dickinson used pentameter very sporadically, usually only to evoke patriarchal concepts such as Christianity, or issues of authority—which illustrates her own wrestling with patriarchy in trying to assert her identity as a poet. Finch notes:

> By Dickinson's time, iambic pentameter had been in standard and nearly uninterrupted use for five hundred years. Milton's blank verse in *Paradise Lost* had given iambic pentameter an even heavier weight of authority than it had carried after Chaucer, Spenser and Shakespeare. . . . Dickinson chose to gnaw at iambic pentameter mostly from a strict metrical framework in the mid-nineteenth century, rather than radically loosening meter as did her contemporary, Whitman. As a male poet, Whitman could appear to disregard accentual-syllabic prosody, the entire basis of the entire patriarchal poetic

tradition since Chaucer. As a female poet . . . Dickinson could proba-
bly not have done so without making her verse impossible—leaving
it with no "authority" at all. (17–18)

In *The Ghost of Meter,* Finch points out that a seldom-noted conse-
quence of the Modernist rejection of traditional form was a rejec-
tion of most of the entire history of American women's poetry.
Male Modernists such as Pound directly associated rhyme meter
with sentimentality—another trait verboten in Modernist aesthetics
—and frequently equated such poetry with women's poetry. There
is, in fact, some truth to this association; the nineteenth-century
women's tradition of poetry (along with much poetry by men)
stressed direct expression of emotion in strict forms, an expression
that often crossed the line from sentiment to sentimentality. Finch
notes: "The fact that women's poetry was associated with sentimen-
tality, and sentimentality with formal verse, meant that the full force
of the [M]odernist revolution—both its misogyny and its hatred of
the traditional and bourgeois—was brought to bear on the crafted
female lyric" (91). The result for Modernist women poets such as
Moore, H.D., and Amy Lowell: "The price of participation in the
new movements was the abandonment of the whole female poetic
tradition" (90).

Many women poets later in the twentieth century, writing as fem-
inism emerged as a political movement, continued the Modernist
aversion to traditional form. As Alicia Suskin Ostriker has noted, vir-
tually an entire generation of feminist poets, coming of poetic age
in the 1950s and 1960s, make open form a fundamental part of their
aesthetic, using free verse to explore the large- and small-scale im-
pacts of oppression on women's lives. The feminists' choice of free
verse differs from the Modernists'; instead of associating meter and
rhyme with bourgeois values, they associate them with the long, pa-
triarchal tradition of male poetry (a concern that Dickinson shared
a century ago, as noted earlier). Adrienne Rich's shift from her early
New Critical formality to free verse in 1963 is characteristic; since
then, she has written almost exclusively in free verse, and she is not

alone in her generation. Other poets such as Margaret Atwood, Kathleen Fraser, Judy Grahn, Erica Jong, June Jordan, Denise Lever- tov, Diane Wakoski, and others make free verse a central part of their aesthetic.

The double influence of Modernist and feminist poetry has posed unusual problems for women who want to write in traditional form—both for women who consciously associate themselves with the Expansive poetry movement, and women who are part of a broader shift to traditional form (which the Expansive poetry move- ment both reflects and helps continue). Such poets are faced with re- fusing an aesthetic with the cultural prestige of both Modernism and feminism—a potentially difficult refusal, given that many con- temporary women formalist poets share the feminist values of their free-verse foremothers. How can feminist poets consciously align themselves with forms and traditions so thoroughly devalued?

That is the question that Finch's anthology, *A Formal Feeling Comes,* attempts to answer. The anthology includes poems by 60 poets, from well-known writers such as Rita Dove, Molly Peacock, and Anne Waldman to lesser-known poets such as Rhina Espaillat and Sarah Gorham, along with short essays by each explaining her relationship to traditional form. As Finch's introduction notes, these poets are "from all over the poetic map" (3); the collection represents tremendous diversity in terms of the themes, styles, and personal and political background of the poets, and they utilize traditional form for a number of different reasons. Significantly, however, these poets show—individually and collectively—that there is no neces- sary incompatibility between innovative women's poetry and tradi- tional form.

One of the most common reasons that these poets choose tradi- tional form is also the most obvious: traditional form, because it re- quires adherence to definite, strict rules of meter, rhyme, and stanza structure, poses a significant artistic challenge—and can create a musical richness unavailable to poets working in open forms. Taken as a whole, the poets are attempting to reclaim a large heritage of women's poetry that has largely been devalued—ironically, by women as well as men, by feminists as well as misogynists. And they are reclaiming this tradition not out of nostalgia, but out of the (ironically Modernist) desire to "make it new," in a way that can easily be described as feminist; "the long tradition of women's formal poetry is evolving once again," Finch notes (3). And *A Formal Feeling Comes* accomplishes its task well. The range of forms included is impressively broad, as are the themes those forms express; the poems are mostly a pleasure to read, and the essays by the poets are often illuminating. More importantly, it demonstrates indeed that the rich tradition of women's formal poetry has evolved through the twentieth century.

If Steele and Finch examine Modernism in depth, Dana Gioia and Frederick Turner focus more on the contemporary legacy of Modernist thought about poetry. Gioia's criticism, collected in *Can Poetry Matter? Essays on Poetry and American Culture* (1992) and extended in recent uncollected essays, focuses on poetry's place in American culture; the relationship between poetry and criticism; and neglected poets who deserve greater recognition. Turner's criticism, collected in five books, critiques the contemporary Postmodern theoretical establishment, exploring the implications of Expansive poetry for Postmodern thought and art.

A unifying theme of Gioia's essays is the conviction that the university, which has become the dominant patron of poetry in the past half-century, is failing in its stewardship, and that significant changes are needed. Gioia makes this case most pointedly in the title essay of *Can Poetry Matter?*, its most famous (or notorious), which addresses the subject of poetry's relevance in contemporary culture. Gioia's conclusion: poetry has become enclosed in a professional subculture that has little relevance. Although there is more poetry published today than at any point in American history, Gioia argues that poetry has mainly become a self-enclosed subculture of American society associated with universities. He asserts that during the Modernist period, contemporary poetry was an art form that literate people read often, in magazines and anthologies if not in books, but that today's average, educated person does not read poetry.

As both a symptom and a cause of poetry's isolation, Gioia cites the migration of poets to the university and the attendant pressure to publish or perish. This pressure, he suggests, shifts poets' attention from writing to be read toward writing to gain tenure, apparently no longer caring if anyone reads their work:

> the proliferation of literary journals and presses over the past thirty years has been a response less to an increased appetite among the public than to the desperate need of writing teachers for professional validation. Like subsidized farming that grows food no one wants, a poetry industry has been created to serve the interests of the producers and not the consumers. And in the process the integrity of the art has been betrayed. (10)

Gioia believes that rigorous criticism, in the form of selective anthologies and candid reviews, is essential for the transmission of poetry to a general audience, and he argues that poetry has traded honest criticism for networking and boosterism.

In the title essay, Gioia calls for more honest criticism, in both reviews and anthologies (which he says "should not be used as pork barrels for the creative writing trade" [23]); poetry readings that include the work of writers other than the reader, and which make use of other art forms, such as jazz, to attract a more varied audience; teaching methods that emphasize performance of poetry over critical analysis to show students the art's sensual pleasures; and greater use of radio for the performance of poetry. These changes, Gioia suggests, would help shake up the university's "stifling bureaucratic etiquette that enervates the art. These [academic] conventions may once have made sense, but today they imprison poetry in an intellectual ghetto. It is time to experiment, time to leave the well-ordered but stuffy classroom, time to restore a vulgar vitality to poetry and unleash the energy now trapped in the subculture" (24).

Much of the rest of *Can Poetry Matter?* and Gioia's uncollected critical prose is devoted to exploring related questions about the university's stewardship of poetry. Gioia's essays about Robinson Jeffers, Weldon Kees, Ted Kooser, and Henry Wadsworth Longfellow in *Can Poetry Matter?* and elsewhere show what can happen to strong poets whose achievements fall outside the avant-garde poetic lineage from Modernism to Postmodernism that university critics champion (Helen Vendler, beginning with Stevens, represents the academic establishment's conservative wing, while Marjorie Perloff, since her shift to the "poetics of indeterminacy," occupies the radical wing; Ashbery represents their common ground). Without academic critics championing their work, such poets are mostly neglected and unread.

Gioia's discussion of Jeffers is characteristic. "No major American poet has been treated worse by posterity than Robinson Jeffers. . . . Academic interest in Jeffers remains negligible. No longer considered by critics prominent enough to attack, he is now ignored" (48). During his lifetime, Jeffers was at odds with Modernist aesthetics in his insistence on fierce moral clarity and vivid narrative, and as the New Critical consensus about the ideal poem hardened into an orthodoxy that still shadows readings of Modernism, Jeffers's reputation simply withered. (Arguably, the only poet at odds with Modernist orthodoxy to survive unscathed was Frost.) As Gioia notes:

> [Jeffers's poetry] states its moral propositions so lucidly that the critic has no choice but to confront its content. The discussion can no longer be confined within the safe literary categories of formal analysis—internal structure, consistency, thematics, tone, and symbolism—that still constitute the overwhelming majority of all academic studies. . . . But Jeffers's poet independence came at the price of being banished from the academic canon, where the merits of a Modernist are still mostly determined by distinctiveness of stylistic innovation and self-referential consistency of vision. (49–51)

Jeffers does not go entirely unread, of course. As Vendler, writing about Jeffers at the same time as Gioia (the occasion was the publication of *Rock and Hawk,* a volume of Jeffers's selected poetry edited by Hass), notes, "Jeffers is periodically resurrected . . . [but] remains, it seems to me, a finally unsatisfying poet—coarse, limited and defective in self-knowledge" (52). In short, Jeffers's status as a poet is not entirely settled. But Vendler, steeped as she is in Wallace Stevens and the Modernist canon, is not likely to praise a poet such as Jeffers.

Instead, as Gioia notes, Jeffers "is the unchallenged laureate of environmentalists," with a significant non-academic readership. A similar status has come to Weldon Kees, whom Gioia discusses at length in *Can Poetry Matter?* and a recent uncollected essay, "The Cult of Weldon Kees." After disappearing in 1955, largely a neglected writer, Kees gained a significant readership among poets and artists who champion his work, but remains unmentioned in most scholarly histories of American poetry. (A significant exception is *Unending Design: The Forms of Postmodern Poetry* by Joseph M. Conte, which includes discussion of Kees's modeling the form of some of his poems on the musical style of the fugue—a group of poems which has exerted significant influence on Gioia's own poetry, as "Lives of the Great Composers" from *Daily Horoscope* demonstrates.) In "The Cult of Weldon Kees," Gioia discusses the large split between writers of poetry and the university-based critics who largely determine the poetic canon:

> The disparity between the legion of imaginative writers who admire Kees's work and paucity of academic interest demonstrates that there is now something out of joint between the worlds of poets and literary critics. One wonders how much real dialogue about modern poetry now goes on between writers and scholars—even those teaching in the same university departments. The administrative division between English and Creative Writing departments found in most large universities has become symbolic of a deeper schism in sensibility, taste, attitudes, and parlance in literary culture. Poets and theorists not only share no common sense of purpose; they increasingly lack a common language in which to discuss their differences. (10)

This discussion points to Gioia's deep sense of disappointment with the contemporary university's custodianship of poetry.

Expansive poetry is itself a response to this sense of disillusionment about the university—a response that goes far beyond Gioia, and which he articulates in several essays, most notably "Notes on the New Formalism" and "The Poet in an Age of Prose." Because those essays form two of the central theoretical documents of Expansive poetry, I have discussed them at length elsewhere in this book, and there is little need to repeat their arguments here. However, they both extend Gioia's ideas about canon revision, the poet's place in contemporary culture, and the aesthetic possibilities for contemporary poetry.

As a critic, Turner may be the most innovative of the Expansive poets. For instance, Turner's 1983 essay, "The Neural Lyre," written with the psychologist Ernst Poppel, drew on research into the biological basis of meter. The essay argued that most metered poetry— in various cultures—has an average line-duration of three seconds, which correlates to the brain's three-second short-term memory system, suggesting that poetic meter has an evolutionary, biological basis. That essay appeared in *Poetry* and won the magazine's prestigious Levinson Prize, an award usually given to poems.

Turner later collected "The Neural Lyre" in *Natural Classicism,* the first in a remarkable series of books on critical theory in which Turner draws on chaos theory, evolution, and other research in the sciences to develop a comprehensive view of aesthetics and human culture. Turner argues that classical aesthetics are rooted in evolution. In the context of contemporary literary theory, Turner's work is truly groundbreaking in its development of alternative perspectives on art, human cultures, and the sciences. While a comprehensive discussion of Turner's theoretical work is better made elsewhere (see my "Natural Classicism and Constructive Postmodernism," *The Tennessee Quarterly,* Fall 1995), a brief summary of his major books is necessary. *Natural Classicism,* Turner's first major book, establishes the foundation of his perspective. Turner examines recent developments in sociobiology and evolution, brain theory, chaos theory, and other scientific fields to develop a scientific basis for traditional aesthetics. His essay, "The Neural Lyre," is a prime example of this basis. In other contexts, Turner draws analogies between chaos theory and the fundamental traditions of aesthetics—such as the metrical foot in poetry—and suggests that both produce entirely unanticipated complexities.

Turner's second significant book, *Beauty: The Value of Values*, delves deeply into the biological basis of beauty, suggesting that human aesthetic response is an evolutionary development that yields certain biological advantages—not the least of which is the further development of the human brain itself, a process that sociobiologists call "gene-culture co-evolution." Turner expands these and other insights in two essay collections published in 1991, *Tempest, Flute and Oz* and *Rebirth of Value*, which extend his ideas to such realms as education, ecology, and the future of human society.

Turner's third major book, *The Culture of Hope*, is an ambitious extension of his ideas into the realm of cultural criticism, in which he critiques in depth the theoretical and artistic mainstream of Modernism and Postmodernism. In this book, he calls the avant-garde an exhausted mode of thinking, useless for guiding humanity's future developments:

> Since the intellectual underpinnings of contemporary avant-garde theory can no longer be maintained, it has lost its capacity to grow and develop in a way that might serve artists with animating ideas. Nevertheless, those avant-garde premises, elaborated over the last eighty years or so by Modernist and Postmodernist art theorists, social critics, and philosophers, are at present accepted without question by most contemporary artists, who often have only a dim and half-consciousness of what underlies the doctrine, and no real notion of the evidence originally brought to prove it or the argumentation by which it reached its conclusions. (26)

Turner instead notes and advocates an emerging return to traditional modes in the arts: to rhyme, meter, and narrative in poetry; to representation in painting; to tonality in music. And he argues that there is no necessary contradiction between traditional form and innovative art. Instead, he insists that in the Postmodern age, the traditional distinctions between liberals and conservatives are no longer valid, preferring to call the artists he advocates "the radical center":

> art must be committed to no existing political program or part,

though imaginatively it must be able to empathize with all such programs. . . . Though the deep genres and themes of art are traditional, they have a vitality and eternal generativeness that makes them the only final resources against the ossification of social roles and the hardening of political dogma. (10–11)

This is the heart of what the philosopher David Ray Griffin calls "constructive Postmodernism."

The work of Steele, Finch, Gioia and Turner is only part of the Expansive critique of Modernism and Postmodernism; other poets in the movement have contributed thoughtful discussions to this dialogue as well. I focus on these four because their ideas frame significant aspects of the debate, and go beyond denunciation of the mainstream of Modernism and Postmodernism to suggest new directions and genuine alternatives that at once reflect the history of American poetry in the twentieth century and a way past the deconstructive impasse to which that history has brought us. As Gioia has noted, there will undoubtedly be further developments in the evolution of both Expansive poetry and Postmodernism. But one concluding point is clear: Expansive poetry is at once part of Postmodernism and a challenge to it. In the context of Postmodernism, Expansive poetry demonstrates that tradition is always with us, quite like a ghost, haunting us in ways we do not expect, by helping to lead us toward the future.

3

Still Waters

Gioia, Mason, McDowell, Salter

One of the pleasures of poetry is its linguistic economy and sub-tlety—the way that a poem can explore a subject with a musical intensity and brevity that other genres cannot muster. This lyric quality is one of poetry's oldest aspects, owing to poetry's common lineage with song; lyricism offers pleasures in itself, as I argue in chapter V. But well-crafted lyricism—a beautiful surface—can serve other ends as well, particularly for narrative. While certain traditions of narrative poetry, particularly the epic, draw their power more from the events of the story itself, other traditions delve through a calm, beautiful surface into darker, deeper aspects of human experience.

In the twentieth century, the strongest practitioners of this kind of quiet narrative are Robert Frost and Edwin Arlington Robinson. Both poets probe daily human experience in elegantly crafted short and mid-length poems. Their poems are often about unremarkable people or events, but they open up deeper insight into human experience, insights made deeper by their poems' haunting music.

In varying ways, the four poets under discussion in this chapter all use beautiful surfaces to explore deeper human stories and subjects. Dana Gioia uses a wide range of lyric styles to probe the elegiac themes of family, love and mortality. David Mason's poems re-create the voices of numerous characters in taking an intimate measure of American history. Robert McDowell's best poems skillfully imagine entire human lives and the small but profound moments that make up those lives. And Mary Jo Salter crafts an especially graceful lyricism in the service of complex narrative portraits and character studies.

Full Potential: Dana Gioia

In his early essay on the Expansive poets, Robert McPhillips suggests that Dana Gioia (born 1950) "is the poet who most fully realizes the potential" of the Expansive poetry movement (327). Given the range that Gioia covers in his two books of poetry, *Daily Horoscope* (1986) and *The Gods of Winter* (1991), as well as his essay collection, *Can Poetry Matter?: Essays on Poetry and American Culture* (1992), this judgment seems valid.

Gioia's range, in both style and subject, is unusually broad. In his lyric poems, he works equally well in free verse and traditional forms, and in fact merges them in many cases; he works hard to give his metrical poems the colloquial quality of the best free verse, while his classically-trained ear gives his free verse a sure sense of rhythm that approaches a formal measure. Also, some of his most distinctive poems (such as "Lives of the Great Composers" from *Daily Horoscope*) are formal experiments of his own devising, based on neither a metrical form nor free verse, but on forms of music. Within the lyric form, his subjects range from short portraits of the world of work ("Men After Work") to historical poems ("A Short History of Tobacco," "My Secret Life") to music ("Bix Beiderbecke"). But Gioia is not limited to lyric: apart from the mid-length narratives of *The Gods of Winter,* he has also written numerous shorter poems that make use of narrative elements and dramatic personae.

And, just as his free and traditional verse complement each other, so do Gioia's lyric and narrative poetry; he has the ability to sketch out character and story with great economy in short poems, while his longer poems—especially "Counting the Children"—develop deep and beautiful meditations on their subjects.

Though he works in a wide range of forms and modes, Gioia's work features a concern that spans its stylistic diversity: probing beneath the surface of middle-class life. By itself, of course, this is not a unique subject; it has been a staple of American poetry since Confessionalism, and practically became dogma in the first-person, free-verse workshop lyric. And Gioia, to be fair to his critics, does not always break the clichés of middle-class poetry; his widely-praised "Cruising with the Beach Boys" is little different from hundreds of other workshop poems from the 1970s or 1980s, save for its use of rhyme and meter. Here are the concluding two stanzas:

> Some nights I drove down to the beach to park
> And walk along the railings of the pier.
> The water down below was cold and dark,
> The waves monotonous against the shore.
> The darkness and the mist, the midnight sea,
> The flickering lights reflected from the city—
> A perfect setting for a boy like me,
> The Cecil B. DeMille of my self-pity.

> I thought by now I'd left those nights behind,
> Lost like the girls that I could never get,
> Gone with the years, junked with the old T-Bird.
> But one old song, a stretch of empty road,
> Can open up a door and let them fall
> Tumbling like boxes from a dusty shelf,
> Tightening my throat for no reason at all
> Bringing on tears shed only for myself. (5–6)

Gioia's admirers praise the ironic self-mockery of the first stanza, and it does effectively undercut the sentimentality of the poem's theme. The final stanza, however, opens the floodgates: the speaker's throat tightens for "no reason at all," the tears "shed only for myself," privately, some adolescent angst recalled but not clarified.

Gioia's most distinctive work is much better than "Cruising with the Beach Boys." He explores middle-class life from a broader range of perspectives than most contemporary poets. That diversity of perspectives, in fact, is a central feature of *Daily Horoscope*. It contains the majority of his poems on unusual subjects (the pornographic memoirs of a Victorian gentleman, the title sequence modeled after newspaper horoscopes, and the early history of tobacco in America), and Gioia carefully organizes this diversity into a nuanced exploration of his subject.

A central example of his technique is "In Cheever Country." Here is the second half of the poem:

> If there is an afterlife, let it be a small town
> gentle as this spot at just this instant.
> But the car doors close, and the bright crowd,
> unaware of its election, disperses to the small
> pleasures of the evening. The platform falls behind.
>
> The train gathers speed. Stations are farther apart.
> Marble staircases climb the hills where derelict estates
> glimmer in the river-brightened dusk.
> Some are convents now, some orphanages,
> these palaces the Robber Barons gave to God.
>
> And some are merely left to rot where now
> broken stone lions guard a roofless colonnade,
> a half-collapsed gazebo bursts with tires,
> and each detail warns it is not so difficult
> to make a fortune as to pass it on.
>
> But splendor in ruins is splendor still,
> even glimpsed from a passing train,
> and it is wonderful to imagine standing
> in the balustraded gardens above the river
> where barges still ply their distant commerce.
>
> Somewhere upstate huge factories melt ore,
> mills weave fabric on enormous looms,

and sweeping combines glean the cash-green fields.
Fortunes are made. Careers advance like armies.
But here so little happens that is obvious.

Here in the odd light of a rainy afternoon
a ledger is balanced and put away,
a houseguest knots his tie beside a bed,
and a hermit thrush sings in the unsold lot
next to the tracks the train comes hurtling down.

Finally it's dark outside. Through the freight houses
and oil tanks the train begins to slow
approaching the station where rows of travel posters
and empty benches wait along the platform.
Outside a few cars idle in the sudden shower.

And this at last is home, this ordinary town
where the lights on the hill gleaming in the rain
are the lights that children bathe by, and it is time
to go home now—to drinks, to love, to supper,
to the modest places which contain our lives. (20–21)

This is a lengthy quotation, but necessary because the poem exemplifies many aspects of Gioia's work. The poem's subject is consistent with the poet's larger concern with middle-class life, but he does not approach the subject from the standpoint of autobiography—even though the poem is spoken by a voice that identifies itself as "I." Instead, the poem, written in loose blank verse, incorporates material from John Cheever's fiction about the Hudson Valley bedroom communities that orbit, sometimes at a far distance, New York City.

The poem is set on the long train ride out of the city to the suburbs, sometimes an hour away or more. Its speaker, presumably a white-collar executive in the city, observes the countryside passing outside the train window. He notes the landscape's history, ruined shrines erected by the previous century's tycoons, and the landscape's beauty. He is also conscious of the darker side of this capitalist landscape, both the invisible physical work of business that executives in their offices sometimes miss ("Somewhere upstate huge factories melt ore,/mills weave fabrics on enormous looms") and the subtle toll that devotion to business exacts on its executives ("Careers advance like armies./But here so little happens that is obvious.") Then the speaker observes the bright present, the reason he goes to work: "it is time/to go home now—to drinks, to love, to supper,/to the modest places which contain our lives." He has arrived in his own "modest place," where the love and comfort of family await.

This poem is distinctive for several reasons. Perhaps most obvious is its tone of quiet celebration of middle-class life. It is more common for poets to attack the problems of middle-class life, either loudly (W.D. Snodgrass, Anne Sexton) or, more recently, with a quiet whine (Stephen Dunn, Jonathan Holden). This speaker, however, arrives home to a quiet happiness, despite his consciousness of the costs—physical and spiritual—of the capitalist system in which he is employed. The poem is complicated, suggesting that modest happiness is possible even with knowledge of the middle class's dark side. The speaker seems to have found peace, but has no illusions about the life he lives.

Also integral to the poem's distinctiveness is its form, both in terms of prosody and narrative. Its blank verse measure establishes a regular, but unobtrusive, background to let the poem's story and meditations unfold. The last stanza, especially, has a quiet epigrammatic quality that would be difficult to achieve in free verse. The poem's appropriation of a figure from prose fiction is also unusual in the history of recent American poetry, and gives the poem a useful distancing from the personal to the general; though its setting is recognizably New York, the suburban landscape of houses on well-lit streets it describes could be found in any region of the country. The poem's use of a Cheeveresque speaker also celebrates the work of that neglected writer, who also explores the light and dark sides of middle-class suburban life, and—as in Gioia's poem "In Chandler Country," spoken by Philip Marlowe, that hard-boiled Los Angeles detective—explores the borders between prose and verse narrative.

Elsewhere, Gioia has written affectionately about Cheever, and pays him an homage through this poem.

Daily Horoscope, like many poets' first books, is relatively broad in the range of its subjects; though it coheres in its explorations of the economic and personal dimensions of middle-class life, it is in part a record of Gioia's development over a decade or more as he gradually experiments with different subjects and different forms. The book draws its strength partly from its careful organization, with Gioia's core vision emerging through the varied poems. Gioia's second book, *The Gods of Winter*, moves beyond *Daily Horoscope* in its unified focus, in subject as well as theme: it is a book obsessed with the subjects of mortality, generations, and love, especially as manifested in family.

The Gods of Winter is divided into five sections, which alternate between short lyrics and longer narratives. The book's first section is a sequence of elegies for Gioia's son who died in infancy; it sets the book's tone, dark but redemptive. The strongest poem of the sequence—which is full of strong poetry—is the concluding poem, "Planting a Sequoia":

> All afternoon my brothers and I have worked in the orchard,
> Digging this hole, laying you into it, carefully packing the soil.
> Rain blackened the horizon, but cold winds kept it over the Pacific
> And the sky above us stayed the dull gray
> Of an old year coming to an end.
>
> In Sicily a father plants a tree to celebrate his first son's birth—
> An olive or fig tree—a sign that the earth has one more life to bear.
> I would have done the same, proudly laying new stock into my
>   father's orchard,
> A green sapling rising among the twisted apple boughs,
> A promise of new fruit in other autumns.
>
> But today we kneel in the cold planting you, our native giant,
> Defying the practical custom of our fathers,
> Wrapping in your roots a lock of hair, a piece of an infant's birth
>   cord,

All that remains above earth of a first-born son,
A few stray atoms brought back to the elements.

We will give you what we can—our labor and our soil,
Water drawn from the earth when the skies fail,
Nights scented with the ocean fog, days softened by the circuit of
    bees.
We plant you in the corner of the grove, bathed in western light,
A slender shoot against the sunset.

And when our family is no more, all of his unborn brothers dead,
Every niece and nephew scattered, the house torn down,
His mother's beauty ashes in the air,
I want you to stand among strangers, all young and ephemeral to
    you,
Silently keeping the secret of your birth. (10)

This remarkable poem is a direct but dignified elegy for the lost
son. Gioia's predilection for direct emotion, which sometimes goes
astray in his lesser work, here finds a proper balance with the grav-
ity of the subject. The poem depicts a dreary day, with its speaker
adapting an old Sicilian ritual—planting a tree to celebrate birth—to
a new country and a tragic occasion: to memorialize a child taken
by death. The tree is a sequoia, or redwood, one of the grandest
trees found in North America; they grow huge and ancient, as en-
during a symbol of life as one could imagine. The redwood's use to
memorialize a dead child, therefore, is especially poignant; as the
speaker notes, once they nurture the tree from "a slender shoot
against the sunset," it will long outlive its planters and those people
who come afterward, "silently keeping the secret of [its] birth," a
child's death, another slender shoot cut down before it could grow.

"Planting a Sequoia" is unusual in Gioia's work because of its
prosody. Although he frequently writes in free verse, Gioia's line
usually hovers around an iambic pentameter beat; this poem, how-
ever, adopts the long-lined, falling rhythm of Whitman or, more
likely, Robinson Jeffers, whom Gioia has praised—and whose cele-
brations of the California landscape are an obvious precursor to this

poem set in a California orchard. The Whitman/Jeffers line is entirely appropriate for this poem; the long line and oratorical rhythm counterpoint Gioia's simple, colloquial language, giving the poem its beauty. (Interestingly, a critic such as Thomas B. Byers—who has little good to say about Expansive poetry—terms this poem "stunningly beautiful" [407].)

Although "Planting a Sequoia" and other poems in the first section of *The Gods of Winter* deal with the death of a child from a personal standpoint, Gioia also explores the subject and related themes —about adult aging, about family generations, about love—from other angles in the book, particularly from a narrative perspective. "Counting the Children" is one of two long narrative poems in *The Gods of Winter* (the other is "The Homecoming," about a convicted murderer's return to the home where he grew up).

Divided into four parts, "Counting the Children" is an extended blank-verse meditation on relationships across family generations. The poem is narrated by Mr. Choi, a Chinese-American accountant. In the first section, Mr. Choi is sent to examine the estate of a deceased wealthy woman. The woman, a bit unbalanced mentally, had liked to wander around and rifle through her neighbors' trash, and had amassed a large collection of discarded dolls. Mr. Choi sees the dolls, and is stunned by them:

> They looked like sisters huddling in the dark,
> Forgotten brides abandoned at the altar,
> Their veils turned yellow, dresses stiff and soiled.
>
> Rows of discarded little girls and babies—
> Some naked, others dressed for play—they wore
> Whatever lives their owners left them in.
>
> Where were the children who promised them love?
> The small, caressing hands, the lips which whispered
> Secrets in the dark? Once they were woken,
>
> Each by name. Now they have become each other—
> Anonymous except for injury,
> The beautiful and headless side by side. (14)

Mr. Choi wonders if the dolls are emblems of childhood's end, relics forgotten in "dim/Abandoned rooms...staged/For settled dust and shadow, left to prove//That all affection is outgrown, or show/The uniformity of our desire" (14). Shaking himself from his shock at the sight, he turns away and begins his work.

Mr. Choi cannot forget the sight of those broken, dusty dolls. Later, in the second section, they re-appear in a nightmare. In his dream, Mr. Choi cannot get numbers in the ledger he is working on to add up—every accountant's nightmare—and then suddenly finds his family, stretching back for generations, watching him as his daughter's life hangs on his computational skill:

> And then I saw my father there beside me.
> He asked me why I couldn't find the sum.
> He held my daughter crying in his arms.
>
> My family stood behind him in a row,
> Uncles and aunts, cousins I'd never seen,
> My grandparents from China and their parents,
>
> All of my family, living and dead,
> A line that stretched as far as I could see.
> Even the strangers called to me by name.
>
> And now I saw I wasn't at my desk
> But working on the coffin of my daughter,
> And she would die unless I found the sum.
>
> But I had lost too many of the numbers.
> They tumbled to the floor and blazed on fire.
> I saw the dolls then—screaming in the flames. (15–16)

The broken dolls still haunt Mr. Choi's memory, arousing a parent's most profound fear: losing a child. Mr. Choi feels a sense of powerlessness, that he can do nothing to prevent his daughter's death, as nothing prevented the dolls themselves from decaying and breaking. He also feels the weight of generations of family, which in Chinese culture (as in Gioia's Sicilian culture) is elevated above the individual. His fear is one that extends through families for generations. Mr. Choi elaborates on this fear in the poem's third section when, after waking from his nightmare, he re-enacts a nighttime ritual of checking on his daughter: "How delicate this vessel in our care, / This gentle soul we summoned to the world, / A life we treasured but could not protect" (17). He came to accept this fear as part of parenthood: "So standing at my pointless watch each night / In the bare nursery we had improvised, / I learned the loneliness that we call love" (17).

Watching his daughter, now seven years old, sleeping, Mr. Choi in the poem's final section relates a sudden vision about the nature of life and death in families:

> We long for immortality, a soul
> To rise up flaming from the body's dust.
> I know that it exists. I felt it there,
>
> Perfect and eternal in the way
> That only numbers are, intangible but real,
> Infinitely divisible yet whole.
>
> But we do not possess it in ourselves.
> We die, and it abides, and we are one
> With all our ancestors, while it divides
>
> Over and over, common to us all,
> The ancient face returning in the child,
> The distant arms embracing us, the salt
>
> Of our blind origins filling our veins. (18–19)

For Mr. Choi, his certainty of immortality—his daughter's and his own as they take their place in an extended familial lineage—provides no consolation for the parental fear he feels. In the mortal present, immortality is divided and diminished, each person entering and living the same path as their ancestors, and then dying. That the cycle repeats over each successive generation does not change the anguish one feels when facing the question of mortality. If anything, it heightens the fear, because it reinforces the sense of powerlessness that Mr. Choi depicts. This seems evident when Mr. Choi concludes the poem by noticing his daughter's dolls:

Their sharp glass eyes surveyed me with contempt.
They recognized me only as a rival,
The one whose world would keep no place for them.

I felt like holding them tight in my arms,
Promising I would never let them go,
But they would trust no promises of mine.

I feared that if I touched one, it would scream. (19)

The dolls, forever children, again become emblems of his powerlessness. His daughter will not remain a child, will leave them behind, just as children left behind the discarded dolls of the wealthy woman's collection.

"Counting the Children" develops its meditation on the theme of mortality and family on a deep scale. Because of its narrative focus, it adds a dimension to *The Gods of Winter* that might be missing from a more personal poem. Of course, given its context in the book, it is impossible to separate the poem wholly from Gioia's autobiographical elegies; it clearly reflects many of the same concerns. Though Gioia bases the poem on Chinese culture, an emphasis on family across generations also runs deeply in Gioia's Sicilian heritage. In part, this accounts for William Walsh's criticism of the poem: "the reader can be excused for wondering whether it is Mr. Choi who is speaking, or Mr. Gioia" (188). David Mason is more on the mark when he observes that "Gioia may have felt that the . . . openly emotional lines . . . could not have been written without the protective mask of a dramatic monologue" (19). That mask allows Gioia to develop a philosophical meditation on mortality and family in another dramatic context, making the book's exploration of these issues more complex and substantial.

Fear is one of the two dominant emotional tones of "Counting the Children"; the other is love, inevitably intertwined with the subject of family. Elsewhere in *The Gods of Winter*, Gioia examines the subject of love more directly. Perhaps the most substantial exploration of it comes in "Speaking of Love," the book's penultimate poem:

Speaking of love was difficult at first.
We groped for those lost, untarnished words
That parents never traded casually at home,
The radio had not devalued.
How little there seemed left to us.

So, speaking of love, we chose
The harsh and level language of denial
Knowing only what we did not wish to say,
Choosing silence in our terror of a lie.
For surely love existed before words.

But silence can become its own cliché,
And bodies lie as skillfully as words,
So one by one we spoke the easy lines
The other had resisted but desired,
Trusting that love renewed their innocence.

Was it then that words became unstuck?
That star no longer seemed enough for star?
Our borrowed speech demanded love so pure
And so beyond our power that we saw
How words were only forms of our regret.

And so at last we speak again of love,
Now that there is nothing left unsaid,
Surrendering our voices to the dust,
Which has betrayed us. Each of us alone,
Obsessed by memory, befriended by desire,

With no words left to summon back our love. (60)

This is a complex poem that, in certain ways, explores the same
territory as Robert Hass's poem, "Meditation at Lagunitas" ("a word
is elegy to what it signifies"). The poem explores the connections
between love and the language used to express that love. The couple
in the poem fears to use the clichéd language of love, and so avoids
articulating this love at first, leaving it unspoken, even taken for
granted. But love demands articulation, and so the couple falls into
the old, shopworn words—a language against which their actual

love pales, since the human language for love inevitably idealizes it, removing love from daily experience. And so the couple seems to have found both their love and its language diminished: "no words left to summon back our love." The poem's philosophical, blank-verse investigation of its topic is reminiscent of Wallace Stevens, and adds yet another dimension to *The Gods of Winter*.

Though it also features different subjects and styles, *The Gods of Winter* is ultimately a much more focused, unified book than *Daily Horoscope*. Gioia's careful organization is evident in this collection as well, which serves to make the book's explorations of its subjects even more precise. With its mixture of narrative and lyric, free verse and traditional form, the book could in fact be read as the paradigmatic Expansive collection. The book is also among the finest yet to emerge from the Expansive movement—at once further solidifying Gioia's connection to the school and establishing the likelihood that his work will outlive its association with the group.

It would be premature to suggest that Gioia—or anyone else associated with Expansive poetry—is yet a major poet. Two books, even ones as accomplished as *Daily Horoscope* and *The Gods of Winter*, are simply insufficient. In his late forties, Gioia still has decades of productivity ahead of him, and final judgment about his career cannot come until much later. That said, it is also clear that Gioia has already had a measurable impact on contemporary poetry, both in his verse and in his criticism; he is already one of the most influential poets and critics of his generation. His work with form and narrative has been integral to restoring those modes to wider use, to exploring long-dormant aesthetic possibilities in contemporary poetry. Moreover, his essays on poetic form and poetry's place in American culture have been influential far beyond the contexts of the Expansive poetry school. Gioia's achievement, then, is already substantial. Among the many poets associated with the school, Gioia has produced arguably the most coherent and strongest body of work. Final judgment must wait, but if any Expansive poets are still read in fifty years, then Gioia is likely to be among them.

David Mason (born 1954) is a poet of quiet lyricism and narrative skill. In two books, *The Buried Houses* (1991) and *The Country I Remember* (1996), Mason writes narrative and lyric poems in a quiet iambic line, ranging over subjects from family—a number of poems in both books elegize Mason's brother, killed in a climbing accident, while the long title poem of *The Country I Remember* is narrated by two of Mason's ancestors—to dramatic monologues.

The Buried Houses shared the Nicholas Roerich Award from Story Line Press. Though the book is slightly unfocused—an almost inescapable weakness in first collections—it features many fine narrative and lyric poems. Here is "Disclosure," which gives a good indication of Mason's particular skills:

> With blue official flap and legalese
> the state acknowledges an end to what
> began in privacy, in passing glances.
> What I remember of your voice is not
> an issue lawyers willingly address,
> and I've avoided their neat document.
> There was a time when the word "wife" warmed me,
> but as you say I think too much of words.
>
> Many nights I raised my head from the pillow,
> watched you sleeping, wife in a girl's flannel,
> there by the bed your window open.
> Long-stemmed, unnamable flower in whom
> I was lost and saved for ten brief years,
> my rancor can't contain these images:
> your hair lightened to its roots by Greek sun,
> my maps of married pleasure on your skin.
>
> It's strange what we can make ourselves believe.
> Memory saves; recrimination uses
> every twisted syllable of the past.
> Still, with all the errors I acknowledge
> added to those I fail or refuse to see,

I say our marriage was a gentle thing,
a secret bargain children sometimes make
and then forget when the weather's changed.

Lawyers put it another way; they don't know
how small exchanges still take place, of gifts
collected long ago, drawings of a house
we lived in, letters from friends we haven't told.
How separately we stumble on some object,
a book I signed, a scarf you knitted,
and call to tell the other it is there,
wondering if it will be wanted back. (81–82)

This poem, written in an unobtrusive blank verse, explores the difficult territory of life after a divorce. The emotions of such a split are always ambivalent, Mason notes. "[R]ecrimination uses/every twisted syllable of the past," recalling both "my maps of married pleasure on your skin" and "an end to what/began in privacy, in passing glances." The poem's narrator loved his wife, and yet their marriage ended. And yet, in a way, the marriage remains, both in memory and in the occasional discovered object from the past that prompts a "call to tell the other it is there,/wondering if it will be wanted back." That is the fundamental question that "Disclosure" asks: what will be wanted back? The speaker obviously still holds some affection, some love, for his ex-wife; in this way, as well, the marriage persists. One cannot be married ten years and make a perfect break from that marriage; it colors one's life for years afterward. The poem's complex mixture of fondness, regret and bitterness— plus the speaker's all-too-human incomprehension of how to handle this subtle aftermath of divorce—make "Disclosure" an especially compelling lyric.

The Country I Remember, Mason's superb second book, is dominated by the collection's long title poem, but also includes a section of shorter lyrics. This discussion will focus on "The Country I Remember" to illustrate the ways Mason's lyric narrative skills operate on the larger canvas of the long poem. The poem is ambitious, and its achievement equals its ambition.

"The Country I Remember" is narrated by two voices, Lieu-
tenant Mitchell and his daughter, Maggie Gresham. Mitchell is a
Union officer in the Civil War, an experience that colors his entire
life, and that of Maggie, who inherits her father's independent streak.
The similarities of temperament provide a continuity to the narra-
tive, which stretches from the 1850s—Mitchell's young adulthood
fighting Indian wars in Oregon—to the 1950s, when Maggie (now
Mrs. Gresham) is living out her final years in Los Angeles.

The poem is divided into 12 sections, alternating with the voices
of Lt. Mitchell and Maggie. The poem begins with "How We Came
This Far," in which Maggie—speaking in 1954 in Los Angeles, two
years before her death—recalls her family's move from Illinois to
Pomeroy, Washington, still a territory then. This section gives a sense
of pioneer life, when the west was still relatively unsettled, and mov-
ing there was, in a real sense, entering into the wilderness:

> Had my Papa brought us to this empty place
> in desperation? I watched his regal head
> nodding on his chest, the long V of beard
> flowing over his crossed and worsted arms.
> I was the happiest child when he had left
> the farm, but I now prayed
> the night would not destroy us like the lost.
>
> The poets told us that this land was new
> but, though I was a child, I understood
> it was as ancient as the word of God,
> and we were like those wandering tribes of old;
> no one had chosen us to travel west,
> and it would serve no purpose for a girl
> to question choices that her parents had made. (4)

This section establishes Maggie's own wanderlust, her inability to
set down roots, which is a central theme of the poem:

> We came this far, and maybe I could go
> farther on my own. Papa had slowed down
> but wandering was in my blood—and his—

and he would have to understand my going
and how no place had ever been my home. (7)

"Cobb's Orchard," the second section, introduces Lt. Mitchell, speaking in the year he died, 1918. (We never learn Mitchell's first name.) The section's narrative is set during the Civil War, but in a surprising fashion: it depicts Mitchell's troops not in battle but searching for food, since they have run out of provisions. They have to forage, bargain with farmers, and outright steal to stay alive.

> A hungry army's enough to spook the dead
> the way it marches on without a sound,
> only the clatter of our gear and wagons,
> a noise of hoof and boot hemmed in by hills.
> We were in McCook's force, pushing south,
> the western flank of Rosecrans' three corps
> butting General Bragg from Chattanooga.
>
> Two days out of Goldsboro we ran short
> of rations, feeding off the countryside.
> The first day without food my boys made do
> with coffee. After that my colored man
> went out with a sack to gather what he could.
> He caught up when we camped on Willow Creek,
> a heap of elderberries all he'd found.
>
> "We'll feast on 'em," I said. The 79th
> had gathered hay enough for all our horses.
> My company had elderberry juice,
> cooked in kettles and coffeepots for supper.
> My Captain said, "Men, shake out your haversacks
> for crumbs," but there wasn't enough to feed a bird
> and the men fell quiet, looking at their boots. (8)

This section establishes a human dimension to the war, in an immediate and unusual way, and establishes hunger as a recurring image in the poem.

The third section, "All Houses are Haunted," depicts Maggie's restlessness further, while the fourth, "Acoustic Shadows," portrays a skirmish between Mitchell's troops and Confederate soldiers. Then comes arguably the two central sections of the poem: "Leaving Pomeroy," in which Maggie, unmarried and nearing thirty, leaves the farm; and "Boyish War," which relates Mitchell's experience at Chickamauga, one of the major battles of the Civil War. Both sections get the characters under way from unsettled life toward a rooted life, toward a country of their own.

In "Leaving Pomeroy," Maggie decides that she must strike out on her own, an unusual action for an unmarried woman in the late nineteenth century. She has turned down several suitors already, being fiercely independent, and decides she must make space for herself in a world so large it frightens her:

> I see them both receding on the platform,
> Papa in his suit and watch-chained vest,
> Mama veiled as if for someone's funeral,
> the whole town growing smaller till I saw
> it wasn't a town at all, but a few trees
> nestled in the grass of a great dry land
> growing so much wider by the minute
>
> that suddenly I feared what I had chosen. (23)

Despite her fear, though, Maggie feels she must leave.

In "Boyish War," Mitchell himself commences his journey from war to settled life. Mitchell's troops are overrun by Confederates at Chickamauga, and captured. The section concludes with a dramatic scene in which the Confederate commander demands Mitchell's sword:

>   He detailed
> three men with loaded pieces to take aim:
> "Suh, I do not want to use harsh measures."
> I saw those barrels pointed at my breast
> and thought of Mrs. Mitchell and the baby,
> saw my chance for escape would have to wait,
> unbuckled my sword and handed it across.

I felt just like twenty-five cents. They asked
whether my name was on the sword. It was not.
They regretted it could not be returned.
I wish that I had given it to the rebel
sergeant who saved my hide the night before,
but now I had to watch this officer
replace his rusty saber with my own.

Then I felt like six-and-a-quarter cents. (28)

Surrendering his sword pains Mitchell, but he does it out of fear for his family's future without a father.

In the seventh section, "The Country I Remember," Maggie has moved to Portland, Oregon, and found work as an office girl at a hotel. She remains independent, however; when her boss, Mr. Jenkins, asks her to marry him, her response is thus: "I told him I would move to California" (32). The eighth section, "Sojourners," also places Mitchell in Oregon, as he recalls his young adulthood fighting Indian wars in the 1850s, before marriage and children. The section concludes with Mitchell and his men being transported to Libby Prison in Richmond, Virginia.

Section nine, "The Blacksmith," narrates Maggie's acceptance of a marriage proposal from Howard Gresham, a blacksmith who "simply wore me down" (36). She rejects him at first, but then she returns home for her mother's funeral. This prompts a change of heart for Maggie. At the funeral, she sees the time has finally come to set down roots:

The rustle of children filled the wooden pews,
and I heard their shoes on the floor, tapping
and scraping the Lord's floor-boards, and I thought
This is life going on, this is the form
of memory, the way our voices will remain.
I have avoided life too many years.
I have wanted to disappear, and now

at last I am ready for my life to come. (41)

Maggie, who has lost her mother—she never saw her mother again after leaving the farm—now wants to set down roots.

In section ten, "Rat Hell," Mitchell and his men are literally starving in Libby Prison. Despite their weakness, 15 of the captured Union troops, including Mitchell, begin digging an escape tunnel. When the tunnel is complete, more than 100 men escape, but Mitchell is too weak to join them. In the brutality of war, he is left behind:

> "Now, Mitch." It was the voice of Colonel Rose,
> the night of February 9. The boys
> had thrown their blankets down by me, he said.
> "Now Mitch, this is good-bye. I hate to leave
> a man behind, but you know we can't wait."
> He looked a kindly bear with his great beard,
> and I said I was glad to see them go. (45)

This section represents a symbolic break between Mitchell and his earlier, wandering life. Though Mitchell remains a soldier all his life —in his bearing, his mannerisms, his constant storytelling—he turns away from military life to family life. Metaphorically, it is almost as if the military life has left him behind, as the escaping soldiers do.

The poem's final two sections bring the characters to the present in their respective times. In "The Children's Hour," Maggie, now the widowed Mrs. Gresham, takes great joy in spending time with nieces and nephews and their children; she never had children herself. Spending an evening with her niece, Alyssa, she sums up her life thus:

> Alyssa rambled on about her job
> selling real estate after her divorce,
> and while I listened, all at once I heard
> the hoofbeats of the surf come pounding in.
> I thought it was the voice of memory
> crashing and flowing down across the earth,
> and underneath, like roots that probe for water,
>
> and I was moved by everything that moved. (49)

The complex image of moving waves and probing roots—both a kind of movement, though different—sums up Maggie's character. In the end, she "was moved by everything that moved." She has found her place in the world.

Lt. Mitchell reaches a similar summation in the poem's twelfth section, "80 Acres." He has been at Pomeroy for many years, his wife has passed away, and he now awaits his own death:

> I'm getting used to living here in town.
> This is my home. This is my home because
> I say it is. I told you about my life
> so you would know how this place is my home.
> I knew I'd come back like a boy in love
> and build my wife that frame house, room by room.
> I knew that one of us would choose a grave.
>
> And I will rest there when my time has come. (56)

Mitchell, too, awaits his final settlement.

Thematically, "The Country I Remember" works primarily on two levels. The first, and most significant, is as a portrait of its two protagonists, Lt. Mitchell and his daughter, Maggie Gresham. The two characters are quite similar in the trajectories of their lives: first restless, then settled. Both are searchers who eventually find what they seek. Their motivations, of course, are different. Mitchell is very much a man of his time. His travels, first as a wandering youth, then as a soldier, and then as a father striking out west with his family, are characteristic of the latter nineteenth century. By contrast, Maggie is not a woman of her time. Her independence and unwillingness to surrender it through marriage are most unconventional for the early twentieth century. Both, however, come to see the richness of the rooted life, of having a place to call one's own and live, and both eventually embrace this life. Nothing symbolizes this more than Mitchell's concluding observation of his future grave. Despite the differing environments in which they lived, the resemblance of daughter to father in "The Country I Remember" is unmistakable. The poem is a rich, subtle portrait of its two protagonists and their family.

By examining the lives of Lt. Mitchell and Maggie Gresham, "The Country I Remember" takes the measure of American history as well. It touches, unobtrusively, on an entire century of American history, from the 1850s to the 1950s, by depicting the passage of human lives through that time. In that passage, we see the most wrenching conflict in American history, played out in small, individual encounters with courage and violence; we see nineteenth century "manifest destiny" not as abstract ideology but a driving force in Mitchell's family; we see the changing roles for women in society through Maggie's life choices and her observations of other women, specifically her mother and the younger women in her family. Its historical dimension is understated but undeniably present. Its subtlety and myriad levels make "The Country I Remember" a narrative of unusual power and thoughtfulness.

For Mason, the attractions of narrative are clear. As he notes in "Other Lives: On Shorter Narrative Poems," an essay in a special issue of *Verse* on New Formalism edited by Robert McPhillips:

> There are at least two good reasons why contemporary poets might use verse to create characters and tell stories. One reason is that it can rejuvenate their art by compelling them to reevaluate the subjects they write about, to look more closely at lies usually deemed insufficiently flashy or spectacular. By involving us in the nuances of social and individual problems, narrative poetry can address issues beyond the narrow confines of the poet's life, or it can focus emotions too painfully personal to be revealed directly in a lyric. It is also possible that the line has advantages lacking in prose, the chief one being that it contributes to memorability, helping to sustain a literary culture most of us would agree is in danger of extinction. (16)

That is evident in "The Country I Remember," which "has risked feelings of uncommon delicacy"—a phrase Mason applies to Dana Gioia's "Counting the Children" (19). Mason's lyricism in the service of story is a distinctive accomplishment.

Mason has published only two books, but he has already emerged as a significant poet of his generation. Though *The Buried Houses* suffers from the lack of focus that is characteristic of first books (the book is organized loosely by theme, but one could imagine any number of other arrangements for the poems), it has scarcely any weak poems, and a number—including "Spooning" and "Blackened Peaches"—rank among the best shorter poems the Expansive poetry movement has yet produced. And, more significantly, *The Country I Remember*—especially the title poem—surpasses everything in *The Buried Houses*. It is a narrative of memorable characters and great historical sweep, as Mason takes the measure of more than a century through the re-created voices of his family.

Small Moments, Large Stories: Robert McDowell

The greatest strengths of Robert McDowell's (born 1953) poetry reside in its narrative element; they are the same strengths of a good short story, or, in his longer poems, a good novel. Those strengths include engaging characters and plots, a clear eye for human action, and a larger vision about humanity emerging from the story. More subtly, these strengths also include an engagement with the broader history of story; the best narratives, even those adhering strictly to traditional narrative conventions, still add something to those traditions. McDowell's poems draw on, without simply imitating, the example of the three twentieth-century masters of narrative verse: Robert Frost, Robinson Jeffers, and Edwin Arlington Robinson.

McDowell's strongest narratives present plots with ordinary characters leading ordinary lives; they achieve their drama through the small but profoundly important moments that lead to fundamental changes in the characters' lives. This discussion will focus on McDowell's two most ambitious narratives: the title poem of his first book, *Quiet Money* (1987); and his second book, *The Diviners* (1995), a single long narrative.

"Quiet Money," written in a loose iambic line of varying length, is a poem about an unusual subject: a bootlegger who beats Charles Lindbergh as the first man to fly alone across the Atlantic. The irony is that because of the illegal cargo he carried—he flew during Prohibition—he must hide his accomplishment. The poem draws its drama less from narration of the flight than from its close study of the main character, Joe, and his life.

Early in the poem, Joe is the consummate pilot, preparing to fly to Norway for his illegal cargo, gin:

> He scrambles up on the wing, his perch,
> One step from home. The cockpit
> Makes him think of the backyards of boyhood.
> Clearing trees at the field's far edge
> Joe banks to the left, circling a hill,
> And levels out heading northeast.
> He likes that initial turn, getting the feel of it,
> Feeling the earthbound tug slip away.
>
> He imagines gunning for stars,
> But the stars are at peace, in collusion.
> The sun balloons above the waterline;
> The moon drops down to the sea.
> Joe thinks of the money he's flying,
> Of gin crates tacked in a hangar in Norway.
> He thinks of a present for Betty,
> Of the life he's making, up here, among prosperous currents.
> (30–31)

Later, after his return, Joe learns that Lindbergh had beat him across. It is a bittersweet revelation, evidenced by his response to his love, Betty:

> "Lindbergh.
> I never thought he'd beat them.
> Byrd and the others with their cash.
> I knew he was in the hunt, in a quiet way,
> But I never figured this.
> He'll get tickertape parades and medals now,
> Money and the keys to the mayor's w.c.
> Think of it, honey. All that brotherly love." (34)

This incident affects Joe deeply. In one scene in the poem's second half, he gets into a fight with a friend over Babe Ruth: "Joe claimed that there were players in bush leagues/Who were just as good as Ruth but never got the breaks./Willie wasn't buying, and soon they were toe-to-toe" (37). Joe knows all too well the truth of his observation; one needs luck as well as talent to find success and fame. Because of the very circumstances of his journey, fate prevented him from taking credit—fame—for his talents.

Later, near the poem's conclusion, Joe reflects on the kidnapping of the Lindberghs' baby, an event that dominated headlines in its time as much as the O.J. Simpson case does today: "The papers served up their grief like daily bread" (39). Joe concludes that he would not trade places with Lindbergh:

> "Son, you have to lose to win.
> That notion settled in with us
> And we passed it on to you.
> Thank God. You know what it meant to me?
> My daughter safe, first of all,
> And all of it, really.
> I spent so many nights in her room
> Just watching her sleep,
> Convincing myself no gang would take her
> From me—ex-fly-boy, average businessman—
> And suddenly I was happy.
> My life's course felt fair.
> I thought of fame and money, and still do,
> How what we do to get them can make us sorry." (40)

"Quiet Money" is a compelling narrative poem. It achieves its power through several means: its understated but detailed portrait of its protagonist, Joe; its juxtaposition of Joe's story with events of historical resonance, the Lindbergh flight and kidnapping; and the sharp irony that comprises its central theme, a theme of continuing relevance of American culture. It is worth considering these observations in more depth.

The first aspect of "Quiet Money's" accomplishment is its protagonist, Joe, a proud but flawed man trying to arrive at peace with himself. Fate prevents him from taking credit for his achievement; one could not reveal oneself as a bootlegger during Prohibition. Lindbergh's arrival in Paris haunts him. But later, when he sees what happens to Lindbergh—his very fame makes his baby a target for kidnappers, who accidentally kill the child—Joe concludes that his obscurity is a gift, because he does not face the tragedies that Lindbergh does. He recalls actually seeing an anguished Lindbergh: "The look on his face will never leave me—/A mid-Atlantic look, your plane out of fuel" (39). He is content with the turns his life has taken.

McDowell's juxtaposition of a fictional character with an actual historical event adds another dimension to "Quiet Money." The poem captures its time effectively through small detail; the dangers of an extended flight in the rickety 1920s-era airplane; the oppressive influence of Prohibition; and the joy and sorrow the country felt with Lindbergh. McDowell transports the reader to that time through imagining one man's life in that era. While good fiction routinely uses such techniques, not much contemporary poetry— so much of it rooted in autobiography—does so.

The third source of "Quiet Money's" effectiveness is its thematic relevance. The poem asks hard questions about American culture's fascination with its celebrities and the price such adulation exacts. Joe is at first bitter and envious of Lindbergh, but would not trade his own children for the fame that Lindbergh encountered. In a real sense, Lindbergh's baby was the price of his fame. In the United States today, such questions are more relevant than ever. Lindbergh was, unwittingly, a pioneer in creating the celebrity culture that permeates American society today. In a way, Michael Jackson, Madonna and O.J. Simpson are the descendants of Lindbergh—or at least their celebrity is.

McDowell uses some similar narrative strategies—the juxtaposition of individual lives against a historical backdrop, in this case the second half of the twentieth century—in *The Diviners*, his second book. It is a single narrative poem in five chapters. The poem narrates two generations of an unnamed California family—Al and

Eleanor, their son Tom, and his wife Elaine. The poem spans four decades, from Tom's childhood and his parents' strained marriage in the 1950s to the 1990s, when Al dies of a heart attack, a decade after Eleanor passes away from cancer.

Chapter One, "The Fifties," introduces us to the family. Al, who later gets the nickname "Boss," is young, demanding and ambitious, traveling frequently on business. Eleanor grows lonely; one night, when Tom, who is eight, drags his mother to his school's science fair, she meets his teacher Bill. They are mutually attracted, and soon begin an affair. Al grows suspicious and intervenes; he sends some goons to break Bill's legs, and the affair ends. Eleanor leaves home and drifts from job to job, and finally runs out of money:

> She calls again and says she's coming home.
> Al hears the liquor in her voice and smiles,
> And tells her not so fast.
> > "I filed last month,"
> He says to no immediate reply.
> "I asked for custody, but I'll drop it all
> If you agree to fix yourself and stay."
>
> Exhausted, bitter, Eleanor agrees. (13)

In Chapter Two, "The Sixties," Tom, now a teenager, grows increasingly distant from his father as his parents' marriage continues to grow farther apart. In one scene, on their anniversary, Al attempts to reconcile with Eleanor, suggesting they get a honeymoon suite. But when she suggests a hotel where he carried on his own affairs— the staff knows him by name—he grows nervous and cancels. Tom, also, grows increasingly estranged from his father. One night, watching the upheavals of the 1960s on television, he thinks:

> But some nights when he's quiet in his room
> Tom eases up, a silent, grief-grown boy,
> An inarticulate and bitter boy.
> If his dad could only talk it out with him—
> But he is like the Main Street Cinema
> Since 1965—always dark.

> Tom's sense of loss and pain won't dissipate
> As he focuses more and more on TV death,
> So easy to watch bland heroes sprawled in blood. (26)

In Chapter Three, "The Seventies," Tom's alienation from his father leads him to strike out on his own. Drawing a low lottery number, he faces being drafted into Vietnam, but decides to fight induction as a conscientious objector. This drives a further wedge between Tom and Al, who served in World War II:

> Al shuts his study door. He sits up late
> With scotch and smoke and wonders what went wrong.
> His boy, up north somewhere, is picketing
> Against the draft. Where does the kid get off?
> Himself a veteran of World War II,
> He thinks of duty, pride, then flares with shame.
> "If your country calls, then you just have to go,"
> Al says to no one in the thickening room.
> The drink unlocks a barred door in his head
> And Al is uniformed and young again,
> About to splash ashore in France and kill
> For the first time. He flattens on the sand,
> Takes aim and squeezes off some nervous shots;
> A boy beside him drops, and when he can
> Al rolls the victim over on his side
> To see a face much younger than his own.
> The body seems to sink into the sand,
> The helium of spirit escaping it.
> Al thinks of his own dying as a secret
> That some blonde soldier is about to tell;
> He cannot shake the cold that enters him. (33)

Despite their differences, Al—now "Boss," head of his own company —asks Tom to come work for him. Tom does so, but only briefly; he meets a black girl named Elaine, whom his father would never approve of.

Eventually, Tom and Elaine marry and move far away from Al and Eleanor's home—to Ireland, Tom's ancestral homeland, where

Elaine writes a best-selling book. Their departure marks the beginning of "The Eighties," the poem's fourth chapter. The dominant episode in the chapter, however, is Eleanor's death from cancer. A terse telegram from Al summons Tom home to help care for his mother. In one scene, dreaming, Eleanor looks back on her own life. She imagines her arm leaving her body, disgusted with her indecisiveness, and has a conversation with it:

> "You're making fun of me," says Eleanor.
>
> "It's just to make a point," the arm replies.
> "Before I left you never felt enough
> Or finished anything you ever started.
> Remember Castroville, our welcome there.
> I fixed with readiness. My sibling sagged.
> Those workers had a laugh. They sized you up
> And sent us off to pick; you bent at the waist
> And crept along a row of artichokes.
> By noon the insides of your thighs were chafed.
> You walked out aching with disillusionment."
>
> "Please stop," says Eleanor. Her eyes tear up,
> And then the arm comes close to stroke her hair.
>
> "I'm back to stay," the arm tells Eleanor,
>
> And she is whole again, awash in light. (49)

The chapter concludes with Eleanor's death, and a scene—neither of confrontation nor reconciliation—between Al and Tom, who arrive at a truce if not peace. The scene concludes with Tom's rueful admission that he has a low sperm count—inherited from his father—and cannot have children.

Chapter Five, "The Nineties," brings the story into the present. Al dies of a heart attack, and Tom and Elaine must close out his affairs, as they did Eleanor's. Like Eleanor, Al has visions while he is dying:

> In deeper sleep Al dreams a pedestal
> With his bust crowning it. The monitor
> Is there to store and broadcast history

> And all is well with resting now. He slips
> Into a playback of his patterned life,
> Successes and small faces surfacing,
> So many whose luck went back when he appeared.
> The neon word *survival* blinks on, then off.
> The moonlight billows, ghosting through his room,
> Obscuring the family photos on the dresser. (68–69)

Al does not linger. "So like him to hurry even death," Tom notes (70). Then, in the end, Tom and Elaine jet back to Ireland to live, free from the shadow of his parents: "The hills are harder to bear, / Their beauty so intense it wounds the eye, / But the looking cures. The past is far away" (71).

In one sense, *The Diviners* explores territory common to American poetry: the experience of a middle-class family. Few subjects are more prevalent, especially in the first-person free-verse lyrics that are the dominant mode of academic creative writing. *The Diviners*, however, is radically different from such poetry in its narrative, novelistic treatment of two generations of a family over four decades. There is nothing autobiographical in the poem, unless one counts McDowell's transformation of his generational experience into fiction as autobiography. McDowell has incorporated baby-boomer generational markers—a suburban fifties childhood, Vietnam, etc. —into his narrative of Tom's life.

Nothing extraordinary happens in *The Diviners*. This is probably its most Frostian aspect. Mark Jarman argues: "As the critic Vereen Bell has pointed out, one does not necessarily go to Frost for his plots. This is not to say that plot does not exist in Frost's poems, but it is more as a portion of a life, an episode with the rest of the life left to speculation, sometimes certain, more often not. In fact, its very ordinariness is the greatest strength of the poem" (90). This is true of McDowell's poetry. McDowell makes the family (significantly, their surname is never disclosed) absolutely representative of its time. With the typicality of their lives—the driven father, the housewife mother, and the brainy son—McDowell probes beneath the commonality of their lives.

Here, the epigraph from Zecharia 10.2 that gives the book its title is significant:

> For the idols have spoken vanity, and the diviners
> have seen a lie, and have told false dreams.

Each of the characters has "false dreams" in some respect, and ultimately must face the truth about themselves. Al, the father, is domineering enough to earn the nickname "Boss" at work, but cannot command his wife's life or son's respect; indeed, it is his controlling nature that does the most damage to his marriage. He hunts down Eleanor's lover Bill and breaks his legs, yet when he seeks a genuine reconciliation with his wife, his own past indiscretions doom whatever chance he might have. His dying vision of his work overshadowing the family portrait exemplifies this.

In contrast to Al is Eleanor, who initially imagines she can escape a mostly loveless marriage. First she has an affair, but soon realizes that will not allow her to escape Al. "Move in. With Tom, I suppose? And on your salary?" she asks Bill when he suggests they move in together (8). Then she herself escapes, living paycheck to paycheck, hopping from job to job, but returns when she runs out of money. He compels her to stay by telling her he has filed for divorce and demanded custody of Tom, the real joy of her life. Still, she finds a strength she thought she lacked; her dream about her arm, when she is "whole again, awash in light," demonstrates this.

Of all three family members, Tom has the clearest view of himself and his family—without illusions. His "false dream" is of the perfect family, but he learns early that he will never have it with his parents. And later, he cannot have it with his wife, since he is incapable of fathering children. He dreams he will escape his family, but knows he never will. As he tells his father: "There's nothing decent in me left for you,/Though I am my father's son. And that's my curse" (53). Even after his father's death, his infertility—a trait inherited from his father—will remain.

In his introduction, Dana Gioia argues that *The Diviners*, while indebted to the example of Frost, is also an entirely new style of narrative, one that reflects the interventions of Modernism in the narrative tradition. It does so chiefly through its larger structure, which develops entire episodes while omitting the transitions between them. This reflects the influence of the Modernist sequence, which moves indirectly through several parts, and twentieth-century cinema. McDowell, however, preserves the coherence of individual episodes to develop a sense of progression over time. To a lesser degree, "Quiet Money" also makes use of the structure that Gioia identifies. The difference is primarily in scale. "Quiet Money" is shorter, and studies only a single character; as such, it is an earlier example of this mode.

McDowell is a poet of unusual, and increasing, achievement. His recent, uncollected work—mostly narrative poems of middle length —shows no sign of decline. "The Neighborhood" is a violent trilogy about a couple's menacing neighbor that particularly recalls Jeffers; "The Pact" deals with the tragic consequences of a wife's affair. These poems have appeared in journals, and "The Pact" was also published in a fine-press edition. When collected in book form, they should further establish McDowell's body of work as a substantial addition to the small but growing body of twentieth-century American narrative verse.

Beneath the Beautiful Surface: Mary Jo Salter

In a brief comment on her work in *A Formal Feeling Comes: Poems in Form by Contemporary Women*, Mary Jo Salter (born 1954) provides this perspective on her poetry:

> Formalism is one means of "finishing" something. The crude formalist, the versifier, may count himself finished once everything rhymes. The better poet seeks a finish that may employ, but goes beyond, the conventional tools: rhyme, meter, syllabics, stanzas. Poets who move us write not only to relieve the pressure of present feelings but to put an end to them. They write about lost lovers in order to write them off. Even the warm tribute to restless Spring freezes it.

The most anguished elegy is a polished coffin to silence the poet's own heart in.

This the reader opens; for him, for her, the poet's heart beats again. With any luck, readers mistake that heart for their own. What has finished has begun something else.

It's a tired misapprehension, then, that chains formalism to the dead past or to an assumed coolness of feeling. Nothing unsettles us so much—in poetry, or people—as a beautiful surface. (190)

Salter is very much a poet of "a beautiful surface." Her work has a subtle but undeniable formal grace. But her formalism is not merely artifice; beneath the controlled surface of her work is a deep exploration of her subject, whether her focus is meditative, narrative or (as happens frequently in her work) both. In this respect—a subtle but flawless form that probes its subject deeply—Salter resembles Elizabeth Bishop. Also like Bishop, Salter is a sharp observer of the world around her, and her eye responds as readily to scenes of human action as to scenes of place or landscape. Thus, her poetry has an unusually wide range of subject.

Salter has published three books: *Henry Purcell in Japan* (1985), *Unfinished Painting* (1989) and *Sunday Skaters* (1994). The three books are varied in their tone and themes; Salter writes poems about family, historical and gender issues, her frequent encounters with other cultures, and the role of art. Salter works primarily in shorter modes; her occasional longer sequences are also composed of short poems. Amid her diversity of styles and subjects, however, she achieves a larger resonance of story and theme through the careful organization of her books.

Henry Purcell in Japan, Salter's first book, is characteristic of her method. The poems are about varied subjects, but a sense of history suffuses the book. For instance, one poem, "Facsimile of a Chapel," addresses the question of spirituality in contemporary culture, but does so through references to history, especially the history of architecture.

Here is the second half of the poem:

As it always does when I forget
I'm not really a Christian, my heart
flew to my knees. I was praying,
once again, for the soul
of my grandmother. Behind the stained
and glorious glass ("French: 12th century")
calculated to provoke exactly
this genius of heart, or infirmity, which takes
all beauty for truth, out there in the non-
air-conditioned air, the hot
traffic improvised its aimless
music and whole colonies
of artists were being born to decry
the notion of beauty itself.

What consecrates a place? Although
the chapel was largely French and 12th, a bit
of Spain was thrown in, and some 13th,
thinking not of the faithful craftsmen
who fashioned the cross, the glass,
the altarpiece, but more
of the movers who shipped them here
(and more of the significance
of the Curator than the Creator)
it was difficult to feel sure
of a holy presence. But isn't God everywhere?

Or nowhere? In the cold light of reason
(above the stained glass, track-
lights one might find in a modern kitchen),
I thought of that blindered, overbearing knight.
I wouldn't have brought back his crusades,
wouldn't confess to sins that don't
originate with me.
                    Yet knowing of my share,
and knowing I'd never happen, in my own
century, on a better place to look,
I pulled up a chair. (28–29)

This poem is characteristic in many ways of *Henry Purcell in Japan*, which is concerned with finding history's continuing hold on the present. This poem juxtaposes a museum, which is a kind of shrine to history in its gathering of artifacts, with the present: a drab chapel of fold-up chairs and architectural pre-fab mishmash, different styles crudely mixed together. Yet the speaker's very awareness of the different historical styles of architecture prompts her to think about the history of religious faith and her own spiritual beliefs in the present. Though she rejects the idea of original sin, not being Christian, she nonetheless considers her own sins, pulling up a chair. She seems to achieve a provisional faith in something, despite the cheesiness of the setting and her own religious skepticism; such, it seems, is the continuing power of spirituality in human culture, apart from any specific denomination.

"Facsimile of a Chapel" is in some ways atypical of Salter's work, because it is written in free verse. One can hear the ghost of an iamb in her lines, and occasional rhyme, but the poem is clearly free verse. A more characteristic example of her prosody—that continues her investigation of the past's influence on the present—is the stunning "Welcome to Hiroshima":

> is what you first see, stepping off the train:
> a billboard brought to you in living English
> by Toshiba Electric. While a channel
> silent in the TV of the brain
>
> projects those flickering re-runs of a cloud
> that brims its risen columnful like beer
> and, spilling over, hangs its foamy head,
> you feel a thirst for history: what year
>
> it started to be safe to breathe the air,
> and when to drink the blood and scum afloat
> on the Ohta River. But no, the water's clear,
> they pour it for your morning cup of tea
>
> in one of the countless sunny coffee shops
> whose plastic dioramas advertise

mutations of cuisine behind the glass:
a pancake sandwich; a pizza someone tops

with a maraschino cherry. Passing by
the Peace Park's floral hypocenter (where
how bravely, or with what mistaken cheer,
humanity erased its own erasure),

you enter the memorial museum
and through more glass are served, as on a dish
of blistered grass, three mannequins. Like gloves
a mother clips to coatsleeves, strings of flesh

hang from their fingertips; or as if tied
to recall a duty for us, *Reverence*
the dead whose mourners too shall soon be dead,
but all commemoration's swallowed up

in questions of bad taste, how re-created
horror mocks the grim original,
and thinking at last *They should have left it all*
you stop. This is the wristwatch of a child.

Jammed on the moment's impact, resolute
to communicate some message, although mute,
it gestures with its hands at eight-fifteen
and eight-fifteen and eight-fifteen again

while tables of statistics on the wall
update the news by calling on a roll
of tape, death gummed on death, and in the case
adjacent, an exhibit under glass

is glass itself: a shard the bomb slammed in
a woman's arm at eight-fifteen, but some
three decades on—as if to make it plain
hope's only as renewable as pain,

and as if all the unsung
debasements of the past may one day come
rising to the surface once again—
working its filthy way out like a tongue. (59–60)

This poem is written in iambic pentameter with a shifting rhyme scheme, and is more typical of Salter's technique. The poem constantly shifts between the anesthetized memorial to atomic horror —in English rather than Japanese, no less—and the actual remnants of that past that persist in the present, despite humanity's "attempt to erase its own erasure." That instance of the past is a watch that reads the moment of ground zero, 8:15 a.m. This is the object that quenches "a thirst for history," a real reminder of horror—"the grim original"—amid re-created, pre-fab history working "its filthy way out like a tongue." This understated, ironic perspective is reminiscent of Bishop, as is its fluid form; so is its interest in foreign locale (Salter has lived for extended periods in Japan, England, France and Iceland). Its sense of the pressure of past horrors on the present is Salter's own.

Salter extends this theme in her next book, *Unfinished Painting,* which turns its attention to elegy and love of family and friends. The book establishes this theme across several sections; two poems, "Unfinished Painting," and "Dead Letters," in separate sections, are subtle echoes of each other, addressed to Salter's late mother, Lorimina Paradise Salter.

"Unfinished Painting" is a poem about two subjects: the painting itself, which is of Salter's older brother, and more significantly, the painter, Salter's mother. The poem begins by elegizing the boy's childhood, which the painting only partially depicts:

> Dark son, whose face once shone like this,
> oiled from well within the skin
> of canvas, and whose liquid eyes
> were brown as rootbeer underneath
> > a crewcut's crown, just washed,
>
> his body's gone unfinished now
> more than thirty years—blank tent
> of bathrobe like a choirboy's surplice
> over the cassock's stroke of color,
> > a red pajama collar. (20)

As the poem progresses, however, it becomes increasingly clear that its deeper subject is Salter's mother (identified as the maker of the unfinished painting that adorns the book's cover). The poem's subsequent stanzas trace a contrast between the work of the artist and the work of the mother:

> She rarely put
> the final touch on anything
> when he was young. It seems that bringing
> the real boy up had taken time
> away from painting him
>
> (no crime); she'd also failed to think
> of him—back then her only child—
> as truly done, and one child only,
> but marveled as he altered like
> the light she painted by. (21)

Salter insists on seeing the fullness of her mother's life in the painting, even if it was unfinished; but so is every other part of life. Her mother made the child, she made the drapes that stand behind the child, and she made the painting, or part of one, an uncompleted record of the child and the life around him. And Salter has made this poem in tribute, albeit a subtle one, to her mother, who made so much, and lives now in part through what she made. (The poem itself makes no reference to Salter's mother as the painter.)

A more direct elegy to Salter's mother comes in the book's concluding sequence, "Dead Letters." A five-part sequence, the poem begins by noting the mail that continues to come for Salter's mother even after her death from cancer (a death her daughter did not witness):

> The bills, all paid,
> come monthly anyway, to cheer the dead.
> *BALANCE:* decimal point and double o's
> like pennies no one placed upon your eyes.
> I never saw you dead—you simply vanished,
> your body gone to Science, as you wished:

I was the one to send you there, by phone,
on that stunned morning answering the blunt
young nurse who called, wanting "to clear the room."
"Take her," I said, "I won't be coming in"— (61)

Part II recalls her mother's decline, before her body simply disappeared from its deathbed:

Injected, radiated,
bloated, balded, nauseated;
years in an iron wig that ill
fit or befitted you;
then more years, unexpected,

of a cobweb gray you grew
in thanks to covet:
lurching from reprieve to reprieve,
you taught yourself to live
with less and less,

and so did we—
even, at last, without the giddy
vastness of your love,
so painfully withdrawn when pain
became all you could think of. (62–63)

It was not always this way. Her mother had a radiance that her daughter recalls in part III. Eating dinner with her mother, Salter tries to recall her grandmother's laugh: "it sounded like a baby's xylophone, / thrown down a flight of stairs." Then her mother pulls a snapshot of her own mother out of her purse:

"Here, it's yours."
Stunned at how soon my eyes have filled

with tears—how easy it has been
to give a pleasing answer—
you seemed relieved to put to death
a momentary fright not only mine.
Now, your own forever-
unrecorded voice cut short by cancer,

I still find myself asking: dear
as she was, don't you know
it was you I was crying for? (66)

Even in the face of her decline, Salter's mother had a quiet optimism, which Part IV recalls: "'Mary Jo—I think I'm ill.'//Forgive me that I laughed!/It's too late to apologize;/but that you could find it in you still/to register surprise—/that *you'd* hoped to be well . . . /It kept you alive, of course" (67). And now, in the poem, Salter tries to keep her mother's memory alive. Her reason for recalling her mother's life becomes apparent in Part V, in which she draws a connection between the leaves that fall in her mother's garden—tended now by Salter—and the leaves of her life story, which Salter now struggles to gather up:

If you could see your daughter, no green thumb,
tending the philodendron
you sent me when my baby girl was born!
If you could see my daughter: that refrain
twists like a crimping weed, a vine of pain
around the joy of everything she learns.

And yet it intertwines
forever, I perceive, your life and mine.
From time to time, a heart-shaped leaf will turn
yellow and fall—in falling a leaf torn
out of your life again,
the story I must constantly revive. (68)

These stanzas artfully connect personal and family history, as Salter sees her story in her mother's story, "the story I must constantly revive." "Dead Letters" effectively concludes *Unfinished Painting*. The book is in many ways a more intimate book than *Henry Purcell in Japan,* less focused on public historical issues, but it does skillfully trace the impact of family history on the present. To individual lives, family history is no less important than public history; it is, in a real sense, the most pressing history.

Sunday Skaters, Salter's third book, is somewhat uneven. The

travel poems, based on her time in Iceland, are slack and uninterest-
ing (they use clichés like "the usual suspects" and "white as a
sheet"). Other poems, while polished, lack the depth of her better
work. The book, however, concludes with the best two poems of
Salter's career: "The Hand of Thomas Jefferson" and "Frost at Mid-
night." Both poems are essentially biographical studies of their sub-
jects, Thomas Jefferson and Robert Frost. Salter animates particular
episodes in both men's lives to shed light on their character and his-
torical significance. Both poems are intricately constructed in their
organization and use of metaphor. "Frost at Midnight," for instance,
derives its title from a poem by Coleridge that gives the new poem
an epigraph; the title is especially evocative because of the poem's
focus on the end of Frost's life. "The Hand of Thomas Jefferson" is
equally evocative. Its title notes its recurring image, Jefferson's hand,
which emerges in a variety of contexts, all historically significant, in
tracing Jefferson's life and impact on America.

"The Hand of Thomas Jefferson" opens with "Philadelphia,
1776," with Jefferson writing the Declaration of Independence. After
political jostling over the Declaration's wording, the section con-
cludes with this striking image:

> That morning—it was the fourth of July—he'd bought
> a thermometer. Praised after by the Great
> Emancipator for his "coolness" and "forecast"
> in seeing through an end to monarchy,
> the man of science literally passed
> its final hours in silence and the neat
> recording of a rise in the mercury.
>
> The apex came at one in the afternoon:
> seventy-six, the aptest of temperatures.
> Jefferson must have held up to the light
> his instrument, and read it like a vein
> pulsing with the newborn baby's powers.
> "The earth belongs to the living," he would write—
> out of his hands, henceforward into ours. (79–80)

The rising temper of independence is what the thermometer unsentimentally symbolizes.

Part II, "Paris, 1786," jumps forward ten years. After the death of his wife, Jefferson accepts an appointment as Ambassador to France. While there, he begins a relationship with Maria Cosway, a married woman of Italian birth and London residence. In the process, Jefferson breaks his right hand:

> hopping a fence, head over heels
> for her, he trips and falls. The wrist
> of the hand that wrote the Declaration
> has snapped, the right one, never to be set
> properly again. And the pain
> is compounded when—no liberty
> to prevent it—she's ferried home to London:
> Cosway's property, Jefferson's happiness. (82)

The hand never heals, and Jefferson writes Maria many letters with his left hand. But nothing is ever the same after her departure:

> The broken-hearted optimist
> seals the envelope with his broken wrist,
> and closes a chapter in his life.
> For though Maria returns
> for a season to Paris, though she writes
> letters in broken English that burst
> into Italian, as if into tears,
> though they correspond for many years,
>
> September of '86 has fractured
> their time into before and after. Another
> revolution is soon to happen:
> friends on all sides will lose their heads. (83–84)

That revolution, of course, is the French Revolution, a far more radical revolt for democracy that eventually sends Jefferson home for good.

"Monticello, 1826," the poem's third part, shifts 40 years forward. Jefferson is now on his deathbed, and the United States is celebrating its fiftieth birthday. Jefferson, not surprisingly, has broken his other hand:

> The left
> wrist cracks, and when the fingers swell
> importantly, the fatal flaw they spell
> this time is mortality itself— (87)

As he lays dying, Jefferson laments his unfinished work. Slavery is a darkening cloud on the American horizon:

> Once he seemed ready
> to free the slaves in a flash; but his sense
>
> of impotence has deepened, along with debt,
> and unable to compute a way
> to free his own, he has no more to say.
> Unable to conceive a blanket
>
> emancipation, nor a society
> where black and white are knit as one,
> he wraps himself in a "mantle of resignation"
> and wishes, above all, to be free
>
> forever of the subject. His time is over. (89)

Those at Jefferson's deathbed tell him it is July 4, a date he desperately wanted to see, even though it is still July 3; he dies before the date changes.

At the time of his death, the problems that Jefferson confronted during his lifetime did not disappear—indeed, some had worsened—but the greater good of his legacy also remained. This greater good is conveyed in the poem's concluding image:

> But had he watched the exploding
> fireworks, he might have seen unfolding
> millions of brilliant hands. (93)

The image of the hand—emblematic of Jefferson's wise, but human, leadership—becomes especially powerful in these concluding lines. Moreover, "The Hand of Thomas Jefferson" shows Salter's historical sense taken to a major new level: merging the public realm of American history with the private experience of an individual—in this case, Jefferson—in a way seldom seen in American poetry. It is a significant accomplishment, aided by the poem's formal flawlessness. (Each section features a different rhyming scheme.)

Though Salter's work is somewhat uneven, in three books she has written some of the strongest poems of her generation. Her best work combines formal control, intellectual depth, and in her recent poems, an increasing convergence of public and private concerns. In her confluence of beautiful surfaces and deep delving, she seems to have learned well from the example of Elizabeth Bishop, but she has made this approach entirely her own.

4

Bold Colors

Jarman, Nelson, Peacock, Turner

A s I note in Chapter III, some narrative poems achieve a quiet power through their delicate exploration of common human stories and experiences. Other poems work more boldly, seeking out what is uncommon in human experience. Some do so through the complexity or scale of their stories. The epic tradition is one example of this. Such poems depict an entire human culture or civilization under duress and the transformations that result. Other kinds of poems portray individual human lives in extreme circumstances, showing the power of an individual to persevere.

In the twentieth century, this poetry of bold narrative has had a varied lineage. The work of Robinson Jeffers, which presents sprawling family sagas against a cultural backdrop of humanity's decline, is the century's most successful addition to the classical epic tradition. (The fragmented Modernist epic, such as *The Cantos,* is arguably a different tradition altogether because it rejects narrative.) On the other hand, the tradition that places human lives in extreme situations is more vigorous, as the Confessional mode of Anne Sexton, Sylvia Plath, John Berryman, and Robert Lowell demonstrates.

The four poets in this chapter all paint in bold colors, though they do so in different ways. Mark Jarman is a restlessly experimental narrative poet, whose work probes the limits of narrative style. Marilyn Nelson fashions an African-American family history that spans from slavery to the present day. Frederick Turner blends the classical epic tradition with the conventions of epic science fiction to speculate on the future of human civilization. And finally, Molly Peacock brings an elegant formalism to the Confessional tradition, crafting wrenching poems of often striking beauty.

The Human Story: Mark Jarman

Mark Jarman (born 1952) stands, with Robert McDowell, as one of the founders of the Expansive poetry movement's narrative wing. This is not, of course, because he is the only poet working in narrative, but because he co-edited *The Reaper* magazine, which was specifically dedicated to reviving narrative traditions in contemporary poetry. (I discuss *The Reaper* at length in Chapter I.) More important than his critical work, though, is his own poetry, which is among the most experimental of any narrative poet writing today. Jarman's work changes dramatically from book to book, as he explores human stories from a variety of perspectives and in varied styles. Along the way, he has also turned his poetry into a critical statement on the possibilities of narrative poetry. Regardless of the mode in which he works, though, Jarman's focus is always the human story.

Jarman's early work was more lyric than narrative; his first book, *North Sea*, dealt mostly with the Scottish landscape where he spent much of his childhood. The poems of *North Sea* are written in the imagistic free verse characteristic of much work in the 1970s. Here is one short example, "Kicking the Candles Out":

> I have sat below a platform in Scotland
> In a cold room where Sunday school met
> And overhead watched the men dancing.
> Their thighs flexing the beat

Into their waists, their arms curled like antlers,
And their women, as good dancers as they,
As muscular and light, shouting.
Hours of music I can no longer hear
Keeps them sweeping their boot toes
So near the ceiling, with its cracks and rain-patches,
That they graze the lights hanging on chains,
Making them turn in a drizzle of plaster
Slowly as planets, and keeping them turning. (26)

Jarman's work in this mode is skillful. But by the time his third book, *Far and Away* (1985), appeared, this terse lyricism had relaxed into a more open, narrative mode rooted in Jarman's childhood in California. (Jarman's second book, *The Rote Walker*, was published in 1981.) Instead of finding emotional intensity in fragmented images, he is concerned with creating more capacious poems that admit a wider range of emotions and experience. Much of *Far and Away* is straightforward autobiography, but is rendered with a depth and humor uncommon in contemporary autobiographical poetry (as prevalent in the 1980s as cold imagism was in the 1970s). Here is one example that also treats the Scottish landscape, "The Seawall":

Palm Sunday. Nothing worse
than a cold Passion in Scotland.
Back after 20 years from California,
from palm fronds and hearts of palm,
to the treeless town of slate roofs.
In a week He rises again.
I walk by the seawall dusted
by the North Sea's joint-rusting smoke.
Choking you once, it cannot
be oiled out of your bones.
What Mediterranean would enter this place,
treading on sprays of frost?

The seawall raises its own horizon.
I know what it means to hear
sympathy and impotent sighing,

the working of weak lungs, in the surf;
to see the dead pulled under the earthworks,
their white grasp slipping from rip rap;
and the sea coal scattered along the beach
like a trade for the poorest
who bend to it. There is always
a first sea of importance
that the second, like the Pacific,
could swallow with a pang of ice.

At the seawall's back, the maze of living.
A butcher shop stuffy with flesh odors,
its damp walls, porcelain cases.
A church where chalices are passed
dabbed by great handkerchiefs, like snow on armor,
their rims warmed by lips.
And my father's roses in the parsonage garden,
like overturned footstools, 20 years old,
49er, Texas Centennial, Newport News—
the tags lost, the black clods
roughened all over, glittering. (64)

This poem revisits the Scottish landscape of Jarman's youth, viewed
from an adult perspective; its images, which more fully depict the
landscape than the poems of *North Sea*, suggest a story of the pas-
sage of time, both for the landscape and the poem's narrator. For
both, much has changed.

Jarman's more recent—and distinct—narratives have grown in-
creasingly stylized. They are poems that are not just stories in verse,
but are also about storytelling in verse. A good example is the title
poem of *The Black Riviera* (1990), a book that shared the Poets' Prize
with John Haines's *New Poems: 1980–1988*:

There they are again. It's after dark.
The rain begins its sober comedy,
Slicking down their hair as they wait
Under a pepper tree or eucalyptus,
Larry Dietz, Luis Gonzales, the Fitzgerald brothers,

And Jarman, hidden from the cop car
Sleeking innocently past. Stoned,
They giggle a little, with money ready
To pay for more, waiting in the rain.

They buy from the black Riviera
That suddenly appears, as if risen,
The apotheosis of wet asphalt
And smeary-silvery glare
And plush inner untouchability.
A hand takes money and withdraws,
Another extends a sack of plastic—
Short, too dramatic to be questioned.
What they buy is light rolled in a wave.

They send the money off in a long car
A god himself could steal a girl in,
Clothing its metal sheen in the spectrum
Of bars and discos and restaurants.
And they are left, dripping rain
Under their melancholy tree, and see time
Knocked akilter, sort of funny,
But slowing down strangely, too.
So, what do they dream?

They might dream they are in love
And wake to find they are,
That outside their own pumping arteries
Which they can cargo with happiness
As they sink in their little bathyspheres,
Somebody else's body pressures theirs
With kisses, like bursts of bloody oxygen,
Until, stunned, they're dragged up,
Drawn from drowning, saved.

In fact, some of us woke up that way.
It has to do with how desire takes shape.
Tapered, encapsulated, engineered
To navigate an illusion of deep water,

Its beauty has the dark roots
Of a girl skipping down a high-school corridor
Selling Seconal from a bag,
Or a black car gliding close to the roadtop,
So insular, so quiet, it enters the earth. (4–5)

"The Black Riviera" treats much of the same material as *Far and Away:* Jarman's adolescence in California. But Jarman's way of handling this material is markedly different. The poem begins with an external perspective of Jarman and his friends standing around waiting to buy marijuana. The narrator, presumably an older Jarman, regards these stoned boys with amusement. "So, what do they dream?" They dream of what they cannot know, of immersion in life and love that pressures them like deep water. And, in fact, what some of these boys find is exactly what they dream of, but they cannot know that when they are young, getting stoned. Instead, they are awed by a black car "[s]o insular, so quiet, it enters the earth."

With its complex shifts in perspective, "The Black Riviera" becomes as much a poem about narrative as a narrative in itself. The great temptation in narrative poems about adolescence is nostalgia, to lament the lost innocence in youth. But "The Black Riviera" turns such conventions upside down. In "The Black Riviera," these unsettled teens eventually find their settled places, but they cannot know they will; only the speaker does. The poem recreates the giddy recklessness of adolescence, but adds a sense of self-conscious distance from it that the poems of *Far and Away* did not; instead, the adult perspective is front and center, challenging a reader's assumptions about narrative poems of adolescence. In "The Black Riviera," knowing how the story turns out adds an additional dimension of insight: one is more tempted to regard the boys as works in progress, with patient amusement. In this poem, adolescence is a skin to be shed for the greater garb of adulthood. Because of this perspective, "The Black Riviera" resists the romanticism so common to poems of youth. This poem, like life itself, has a more complex ending than tidy nostalgia.

If *The Black Riviera* features a number of small-scale narrative experiments like its title poem, Jarman's next book, *Iris* (1992), is a large-scale experiment. This sprawling three-part narrative poem is an homage to Robinson Jeffers, one of the century's major, but neglected, narrative poets. The homage works on two levels. First, it is written in Jeffers's style—his long, Whitmanian line and his lurid plot. Second, Jeffers himself is a central figure in the story; the book's protagonist is obsessed with Jeffers's poetry, and the plot is structured as a journey to Carmel, Jeffers's home in California.

The book relates the story of Iris, a young woman from Kentucky who discovers the poetry of Jeffers in a college course. She has left her abusive husband and moved in with her mother and brothers, taking her daughter Ruth with her. With her family, Iris scratches out a marginal existence, until violence again drives her away. Her brothers grow marijuana to bring extra money in, but one day they encounter a bad deal. Iris happens onto the aftermath:

> She heard a doglike moan turn human. There they lay, the four of
>   them, face down, arms bound
> Like chicken wings, in the living area. Ruth stood at their feet and
>   said, "That's Uncle Hoy and Uncle Rice.
> That's Charles. That's Grandma," as if making sure she knew the
>   names.
> They all looked scalped at first. Mama's wig, a bloody ball, lay just
>   above her head.
> She was moaning, cut down to the bone by the shotgun blast, but
>   still alive. Alive,
> As Ruth and Iris were, thought Iris. Alive as we are, the two sacks
>   in her arms. "That's Grandma's wig,"
> Said Ruth. Iris saw the woman move. "That's Uncle Hoy and Uncle
>   Rice and Charles,"
> Said Ruth again. And Iris, in the last moment before acting, found
>   herself
> Thanking God for Ruth's sake they had gone to Kroger's. (39)

At this point, Iris flees Kentucky with Ruth and her mother, and they strike out for California. Her destination is Carmel, the northern California region where Jeffers made his solitary life, but they

settle for the moment in southern California after they move in with
Smith, a salesman Iris has met. Still, being nearer the majestic land-
scapes Jeffers depicted so magnificently affects Iris's imagination:

> She read
> Her Vintage paper back of Jeffers and felt his voice, tugging her
>   north.
> The bay's south side was close and curved along a green peninsula,
>   but the northern curve
> Ended in mountain silhouettes. Thus, distance added to the
>   voice—apparent distance—
> And made an answer seem impossible. For Iris, looking outward al-
>   ways ended
> In the short view—the day and day's end. The longer vistas opened
>   up inside her. (58–59)

Though she never marries Smith, Iris remains with him for 20
years and comes to call him her husband. She raises Ruth, who even-
tually marries; her mother dies. All the while, however, she never
forgets Carmel calling her, from the north. She decides ultimately to
leave Smith and strike out for Tor House, the home Jeffers built his
wife Una out of quarry stone. She picks up a hitchhiker along the
way, Nora, who has had a difficult life much like hers; eventually the
new friends reach Tor House. For Iris, it is like coming into heaven:

> Iris and Nora walked to the house gate. The sky came down be-
>   hind the blue tower, pale blue
> And almost white along the seam it made with ocean. The sky the
>   water was reflecting,
> Iris thought, could not be that sky. It had to be some wine dark,
>   purple sky, or cloth,
> Bleeding a blue dye beneath its surface. But what she could not
>   bear at first was how close
> It all was. A few strides would let her lay her hand on the square
>   tower. Its angles made
> Of boulders he had set, each rounded to a softness, though heavy
>   with mass, dense with weight.
> And the stone house equally in reach. She felt the power to say, but
>   only to herself,

She knew reality because it looked her in the face. Nothing could duplicate

The face-to-face regard of something real. (125–126)

And finally, Iris enters the house, home of the man whose expansive narratives about human interaction with that landscape have literally given her life meaning:

Iris held back a little as the party entered the small house. In the side garden,

In the full sunlight sweeping Carmel Bay from here to Point Lobos, a line of iris stood,

Robust, two feet tall, their long petals curling back, lavender, blue, and deep red-purple—

The ocean's color. Yes. She felt a secret lodge with her, to keep, and entered the low door,

The house where pain and pleasure had turned to poetry and stone, and a family had been happy. (126)

This is a moving ending to the poem. After a long life of searching, Iris has finally found a kind of happiness that she had only imagined: the world of Jeffers.

To write a poem in self-conscious homage to another poet is a risky proposition, particularly when the poem is on the scale of *Iris*. Jarman is not simply incorporating Jeffers's influence into his own work, as did William Everson—a poet, like Jeffers, of rhapsodic spirituality in his lines and themes, although Everson is explicitly Christian and Jeffers mostly rejected organized religion. Indeed, one would be hard-pressed to find a direct example of Jeffers's influence elsewhere in Jarman's work, apart from his general interest in narrative and treatment of the California landscape. Instead, *Iris* is a self-conscious re-creation of Jeffers's idiom on Jarman's part, adapting his long line and melodramatic storyline to the late twentieth century. It is as if a New England poet had sat down and consciously re-worked Robert Frost's patterning of colloquial speech across the iambic line to present-day themes. The risk of being overwhelmed by the other poet's style, and simply producing an extended imitation, is great.

For the most part, Jarman avoids this trap. First of all, he has developed a compelling protagonist in Iris; she is an engaging character who is strong enough to carry an extended narrative on her own. Second, Jarman makes Jeffers an essential part of the poem; Iris's journey makes no sense without understanding her attachment to Jeffers's poetry, the beauty of which lifts her from her own dreary life whenever she sits down to read. Therefore, Jeffers is essential not only to understanding the structure of *Iris*—as an homage to the California poet—but to understanding the poem's story and themes in themselves. The poem is both a compelling story in its own right and an extended meditation on Jeffers's own poetry; it is enjoyable as a narrative, and provocative in demanding recognition for Jeffers's example as a narrative poet.

That said, one should also note the limits of Jarman's enterprise. *Iris* is a singular achievement, and "singular" does not only mean "excellent"; it is also the kind of poem that can be done only once. It is as much a work of criticism as a work of poetry in its devotion to Jeffers as a poet. Jarman has not so much assimilated Jeffers's example into his own poetry as copied Jeffers's style, word for word, into a new narrative context. In this respect, *Iris* is as much like a translation of another poet as an original poem; it resembles nothing else in Jarman's work, not even the stylized narratives of *The Black Riviera*. This is demonstrated by Jarman's most recent book, an ambitious sequence of lyrics titled *Questions for Ecclesiastes* (1997), which aims to invigorate the long-running tradition of religious poetry. Here, the example is George Herbert and particularly John Donne, whose Holy Sonnets provide a point of departure for Jarman's brilliant "Unholy Sonnets." Here is Sonnet 4:

> Amazing to believe that nothingness
> Surrounds us with delight and lets us be,
> And that the meekness of nonentity,
> Despite the friction of the world of sense,
> Despite the leveling of violence,
> Is all that matters. All the energy

We force into the matchhead and the city
Explodes inside a loving emptiness.

Not Dante's rings, not the Zen zero's mouth,
Out of which comes and into which light goes,
This God recedes from every metaphor,
Turns the hardest data into untruth,
And fills all blanks with blankness. This love shows
Itself in absence, which the stars adore. (54)

There is nothing of Jeffers's theological viewpoint of "inhumanism"
here; instead, this poem accepts the existence of God and wrestles
with the question of faith and understanding of God, as did Donne
and Herbert, and Hopkins. The "Unholy Sonnets" are a significant
addition to Jarman's work, along with other poems in *Questions for
Ecclesiastes*, because of their themes and their formal departures
from his earlier work, in their lyricism and formal construction.

As the pointed shifts in direction from *The Black Riviera* to *Iris* to
Questions for Ecclesiastes show, Jarman is not a poet content to rest on
his past successes. He has deeply probed the possibilities for narra-
tive poetry in our time, and, in his recent work, has shifted toward a
more meditative exploration of human concerns. The excellence of
his work across a wide range of style and subject make his achieve-
ment among the two or three most important of the Expansive
school. No one is more restless in exploring the full dimensions of
the human story.

A Long Tradition: Marilyn Nelson

Unlike most of the Expansive poets, Marilyn Nelson (born 1946) has
gravitated increasingly toward form and narrative after earning a
reputation on the strength of her free-verse lyrics. Her first book, *For
the Body* (1978), shows the strong influence of 1970s free-verse surre-
alism, as this short poem (titled "The American Dream") demon-
strates:

I want to go shopping
and buy myself.
I want to suddenly turn
american, sold at the counter
by some sleight-of-mind
salesman who'll trap my dreams
and put me in an automatic cage.

I want my face to stop looking
like an african housewife,
my feet to stop dancing to
lost music.

I want to get out of
my VW some saturday afternoon
and walk through some silent glass doors.
I want to pick myself up
in Safeway. (12)

The compact lines and dreamlike imagery so prevalent in the 1970s
are apparent in these stanzas. Poets such as John Haines handle this
style with a high degree of artistry, but it is not Nelson's best work, es-
pecially compared to one of her rare early poems in form, "Church-
going":

The Lutherans sit stolidly in rows;
only their children feel the holy ghost
that makes them jerk and bobble and almost
destroys the pious atmosphere for those
whose reverence bows their backs as if in work.
The congregation sits, or stands to sing,
or chants the dusty creeds automaton.
Their voices drone like engines, on and on,
and they remain untouched by everything;
confession, praise, or likewise, giving thanks.
The organ that they saved years to afford
repeats the Sunday rhythms song by song;
slow lips recite the credo, smother yawns,
and ask forgiveness for being so bored.

I, too, am wavering on the edge of sleep,
and ask myself again why I have come
to probe the ruins of this dying cult.
I come bearing the cancer of my doubt
as superstitious suffering women come
to touch the magic hem of a saint's robe.

Yet this has served two centuries of men
as more than superstitious cant; they died
believing simply. Women, satisfied
that this was truth, were racked and burned with them
for empty words we moderns merely chant.

We sing a spiritual as the last song,
and we are moved by a peculiar grace
that settles a new aura on the place.
This simple melody, though sung all wrong,
captures exactly what I think is faith.
Were you there when they crucified my Lord?
That slaves should suffer in his agony!
That Christian, slave-owning hypocrisy
nevertheless by these slaves ignored

as they pitied the poor body of Christ!
Oh, sometimes it causes me to tremble,
that they believe most, who so much have lost.
To be a Christian, one must bear a cross.
I think belief is given to the simple
as recompense for what they do not know.

I sit alone, tormented in my heart
by fighting angels, one black, one white.
The victory is uncertain, but tonight
I'll lie awake again, and try to start
finding the black way back to what we've lost. (16–17)

This remarkable poem successfully adapts Philip Larkin's "Church Going," another poem of religious skepticism, to African-American religious experience, drawing a contrast between white and black services while asking hard questions about spirituality. God's grace, she suggests, is felt the most by those who have the least—in contrast to today's middle-class churchgoers, mouthing prayers with no fervor. The poem's use of meter and rhyme gives a sharp clarity to Nelson's ideas, which is mostly absent from her more surrealist work.

Nelson has published four other books: *Mama's Promises* (1985), which mostly refines the style of *For the Body; The Homeplace* (1990), in which her interest in form and narrative comes into full flower; and *Magnificat* (1994), which extends, though not as successfully, the stylistic breakthrough of *The Homeplace;* and *The Fields of Praise* (1997), a book of selected poems. This discussion will focus on *The Homeplace,* which is Nelson's best book.

The Homeplace is primarily a narrative collection that re-creates several generations of Nelson's family; a short concluding section of poems focuses separately on the Tuskeegee Airmen, to whom her father belonged. In this respect, *The Homeplace* bears a family resemblance to Rita Dove's *Thomas and Beulah* (1987), in which Dove fashioned a narrative based on the lives of her grandparents. But *The Homeplace* is a distinctive book, and surpasses Dove's book in its formal range. The collection has its share of free-verse poems—which have traded imagistic dreaminess for the bite of colloquial speech—but also sonnets, rhymed quatrains, terza rima, and other forms. *The Homeplace* tells the story of Nelson's family from her great-great-grandmother—who came to this country as a slave—to her parents through an elegant range of character studies.

Diverne, Nelson's great-great-grandmother, was a slave imported from Jamaica. As a woman slave, she caught the eye of her master—a fact that she used to survive, as the poem "Balance" (a Shakespearean sonnet) makes clear:

> He watch her like a coonhound watch a tree.
> What might explain the metamorphosis
> he underwent when she paraded by
> with tea-cakes, in her fresh and shabby dress?
> (As one would carry water from a well—

straight-backed, high-headed, like a diadem,
with careful grace so that no drop will spill—
she balanced, almost brimming, her one name.)

She think she something, stuck-up island bitch.
Chopping wood, hanging laundry on the line,
and tantalizingly within his reach,
she honed his body's yearning to a keen,
sharp point. And on that point she balanced life.
That hoe Diverne think she Marse Tyler's wife. (12)

At times, though, the balance was upset, and Diverne had to go far-
ther to survive. The conception of her son Pomp is a result of one
such struggle, depicted in "Chosen" (a kind of terza rima sonnet):

Diverne wanted to die, that August night
his face hung over hers, a sweating moon.
She wished so hard, she killed part of her heart.

If she had died, her one begotten son,
her life's one light, would never have been born.
Pomp Atwood might have been another man:

born with a single race, another name.
Diverne might not have known the starburst joy
her son would give her. And the man who came

out of a twelve-room house and ran to her
close shack across three yards that night, to leap
onto her cornshuck pallet. Pomp was their

share of the future. And it wasn't rape.
In spite of her raw terror. And his whip. (14)

As the poem notes, however, Diverne, who loved the son this assault
produced, did not regret the act: "it wasn't rape."

Diverne's son, Pomp, grew up into a self-made businessman, sell-
ing groceries and other products like the poem's title, "Coal":

He made a living selling land and coal
as, when he was a boy, he had been sold:

an honest handshake and a signature;
the cash exchanging hands. He owned a store
across the street from Hickman's Negro school,
and shoveled every day onto its scale
as much pride-bright blackness as it would hold.
He speculated well on real-estate.
He made a living.

With three partners, he formed a business, called
The Hickman Joint Stock Company, to sell—
delivered by wagon up and down each street
the groceries almost half of Hickman ate.
His signature is firm, decisive, bold:
he made a living.(18)

Pomp also fathered five daughters. One of Pomp's daughters, Geneva, is remembered in one of the book's later poems, "The Ballad of Aunt Geneva." Here is the first and concluding stanza of the poem:

Geneva was the wild one.
Geneva was a tart.
Geneva met a blue-eyed boy
and gave away her heart. (26)

As the poem—written in ballad meter, alternating four- and three-beat lines—shows, Geneva seems to have inherited some of her grandmother's passion. She killed another woman over a "good black man/by braining the jealous heifer/with an iron frying pan" (26). And she has a relationship with a white man well into old age:

They say, when she was eighty,
she got up late at night
and sneaked her old, white lover in
to make love, and to fight.

First, they heard the tell-tale
singing of the springs,
then Geneva's voice rang out:
I need to buy some things,

So next time, bring more money.
And bring more moxie, too.
I ain't got no time to waste
on limp white mens like you.

Oh yeah? Well, Mister White Man,
it sure might be stone-white,
but my thing's white as it is.
And you know damn well I'm right.

Now listen: take your heart pills
and pay your doctor mind.
If you up and die on me,
I'll whip your white behind. (26)

The sequence of family poems that takes up most of the book concludes with "The Fortunate Spill," which brings Nelson's parents together in rhymed quatrains (a note indicates that the family serves black-eyed peas on New Year's Eve for good luck):

Well! Johnnie thinks. He has his nerve!
Crashing this party! What stuck-up conceit!
Passing his induction papers around;
another Negro whose feet never touch the ground.

His name is Melvin Nelson. In his eyes
the black of dreams sparkles with laughing stars.

Johnnie agrees to play. And it defies
all explanation: she forgets five bars!
This cocky, handsome boy? she asks her heart.
For good luck all year, Melvin says, you've got to fart.

They eat elbow to elbow, in a crowd
of 1942's gifted black youth.
His tipsy bass-clef voice is much too loud.
Hers trebles nervously: to tell the truth,
she's impressed.

I'll be a man up in the sky,
he confides. She blurts out, Hello, Jesus! And they die
with laughter.

> But the joke catches him off-guard:
> he spills the black-eyed peas into her lap.
> *Oh Lord,* he mumbles, but she laughs so hard
> both recognize the luck of their mishap.
>
> And I watch from this distant balcony
> as they fall for each other, and for me. (37)

The final couplet crisply ends the poem, and the sequence; it foreshadows Nelson's own birth, and brings the family history toward the present.

The Homeplace is a compelling narrative collection in the way it recalls the story of an African-American family. It stands as Nelson's best collection largely through its formal dexterity and thematic coherence. In "Sense of Discovery," a short preface to her work published in *A Formal Feeling Comes: Poems in Form by Contemporary Women,* Nelson explains why she was drawn so much to form in writing *The Homeplace:*

> Frankly, I find it easier to write in form than to write in free verse. There's a sense of closure, of completeness, in form which doesn't exist in free verse. . . . The use of form seems to me to be more appropriate for poems about the historical past. . . . As for the sonnets: I've been experimenting with sonnets for some time, and enjoy working within that small tight space. I do not especially advocate formalist verse, though it does, I think, offer more "memorability" than free verse, and a strong sense of being part of a long tradition. (241)

Certainly when one writes a family history, one is enmeshed in a "long tradition"; Nelson's use of form and narrative therefore becomes especially appropriate in *The Homeplace.* The book is an unusual achievement, especially because it was not strongly anticipated by her earliest work.

Self and Love: Molly Peacock

Among the Expansive poets, Molly Peacock (born 1947) is perhaps the best on the ancient subjects of self and love. Few subjects exert as much power over the human self as love, which has the power to elevate and ennoble, or to terrify and destroy. Over four books, Peacock has explored the subject of love in its myriad aspects, developing an ongoing narrative rooted in autobiography and Confessionalism and given a hard clarity by her elegant, colloquial formalism.

Peacock's first book, *And Live Apart* (1980), dealt, generally, with the subject of self-love, treating the process of forming a mature self as the most loving thing one can do for one's self, for one's survival. *And Live Apart* took its title from a stanza by George Herbert: "Surely if each one saw another's heart, / There would be no commerce, / No sale or bargain passe: all would disperse, / And live apart." The book is about finding one's own heart, and enacts that process in part through its stylistic inconsistency: Peacock's mature, colloquial-formal voice emerges only intermittently here. A characteristic poem is "Alibis and Lullabies," a sequence that explores scenes from the speaker's childhood and adulthood in both traditional and free verse, and includes these lines, unmetered but rhymed:

> This is to explain my cruelty.
> This is to explain the cruelty of my thirtieth year.
> Now that I spend all daylight hours awake, and the fear,
> a fear of the world in its globe tangibly,
>
> I can explain it no better than the outside fiercely
> active and not a part of me, is now a near
> steady pulse I hear then don't hear but don't care
> to forget, since it is me and I have changed and the cruelty
>
> comes from fearing to forget an original self. (28)

Peacock's second book, *Raw Heaven* (1984), is a more fully developed collection in which Peacock's mature voice is on consistent display. Peacock uses an intimate, assured tone to explore the vulnerability of human relationship and love, most often in the sonnet form or a variation, as "Cut Flower" exemplifies:

> From the arms and stems of all the others,
> the whole tribe of lilies swaying

as lilies of lilies together, all lovers,
an instinct inside it kept it swaying
away from what it looked to me its rooted
place. Its silky orangeness in the vase alone,
alone and in command of its unrooted
isolated state, was beautiful, for grown
full nakedness right where I could witness it
was beautiful, huge and proximate.
When I looked at it, I saw my better self
in the makeshift kingdom of a vase. In
cutting it, I cut myself from the swollen field,
out of what I was in, becoming alien.
Thus separation was the power I could yield. (26)

This poem, with the flower an emblem of love, evokes the "raw heaven" of the book's title: paradise, beautiful but dangerous, difficult to tame. In love, as in nature, the self's primary power is to withdraw, to hold back.

If the speakers of *Raw Heaven* approach love gingerly, the speakers of *Take Heart* are beaten down by it. *Take Heart* (1989) continues Peacock's work in traditional forms but connects that mode to the Confessional tradition of feminist poetry. Alcoholism, abuse, abortion: all these topics appear in these poems, and the speakers seek to escape these terrifying sides of love—to "take heart" and find peace and solace, as these lines from "The Ghost" show:

The ghost of my pregnancy, a large
amorphous vapor, much larger than me,
comes when I am alarmed to comfort me,
though it, too, alarms me, and I dodge

away saying, "Leave me alone"; and the ghost,
always beneficent, says, "You're a tough one
to do things for." The ghost must have done
this lots, it so completely knows I'm lost

and empty. It returns the fullness and slow
connections to all the world as it is.

When I let it surround me, the embrace is
more mother than baby. How often we don't know

the difference. (37)

This poem offers the speaker little consolation. Other poems in *Take Heart* are even more wrenching, such as "Say You Love Me," which I discuss at length in Chapter II. Some of the book's final poems arrive at a tentative sense of peace with love.

Peacock's most recent book, *Original Love* (1995), continues her exploration of love, and makes that exploration explicitly. It also extends the sense of peace that *Take Heart* found, and is the calmest, happiest collection of poems that Peacock has published. Divided into three sections, the book depicts the intertwined strands of romantic, familial, and spiritual love—all in poems notable for their skillful craft with traditional forms.

The book's first section, "First Love," explores what the people in Peacock's earlier books sought but seldom found: a happy, stable relationship. The section depicts a flourishing relationship, and the female speaker's stunned joy at finding love and happiness, a joy that overcomes the human fear that love will depart. "Little Miracle" expresses this idea simply:

No use getting hysterical.
The important part is: we're here.
Our lives are a little miracle.

My hummingbird-hearted schedule
beats its shiny frenzy, day into year.
No use getting hysterical—

it's always like that. The oracle
a human voice could be is shrunk by fear.
Our lives are a little miracle

—we must remind ourselves—whimsical,
and lyrical, large and slow and clear.
(So no use getting hysterical!)

> All words other than I love you are clerical,
> dispensable, and replaceable, my dear.
> Our inner lives are a miracle.
>
> The beat their essence in the coracle
> our ribs provide, the watertight boat we steer
> through others' acid, hysterical
> demands. Ours is the miracle: *we're here.* (36)

This poem is a villanelle, which repeats certain lines ("No use getting hysterical," "Our lives are a little miracle") with slight variations. It is emblematic of Peacock's characteristic technique: using traditional form with clear, straightforward diction, to explore personal, even intimate, subject matter in a way that lifts that subject to general relevance. In this poem, the villanelle is an especially appropriate choice of form: the speaker is amazed at the love she has found. The villanelle's constant repetitions and rhymes both register the speaker's astonishment, and anchor it in reality: "Our lives are a little miracle." The love is here, and is not departing.

The theme of departure is taken up in the book's second section, "Mother Love." From the mature perspective of a stable marriage, the poems' speaker elegizes her mother. Unlike that speaker's father, whom Peacock portrays as a terrifying and abusive alcoholic, the mother is remembered here with clear-eyed affection. She was far from perfect—the poems never elevate the mother to sainthood —but the speaker's love for her emerges in striking ways. She imagines her mother sexually; explores why she will not have children herself; and recounts the troubles she encounters in making sure her mother is buried exactly as she wanted. "The Fare" examines this latter topic:

> Bury me in my pink pantsuit, you said—and I did.
> But I'd never dressed you before! I saw the glint
> of gold in your jewelry drawer and popped
> the earrings in a plastic bag along with pearls,
> a pink-and-gold pin, and your perfume. ("What's this?"
> the mortician said. "Oh well, we'll spray some on.")
> Now your words from the coffin: *Take my earrings off!*

I've had them on all day, for God's sake!"
You've had them on five days. The lid's closed,
and the sharp stab of a femininity
you couldn't stand for more than two hours in life
is eternal—you'll never relax. I'm 400 miles away.
Should I call up the funeral home and have them removed?
You're not buried yet—stored till the ground thaws—
where, I didn't ask. Probably the mortician's garage.
I should have buried you in slippers and a bathrobe.
Instead, I gave them your shoes. Oh, please
do it for me. I can't stand the thought of you
pained by vanity forever. Reach your cold hand
up to your ear and pull and hear the click
of the clasp hinge unclasping, then reach
across your face and get the other one
and—this effort could take you days, I know,
since you're dead. Let it be your last effort:
to change my mistake and be dead in comfort.
Lower your hands in their places
on your low mound of stomach and rest, rest,
you can let go. They'll fall
to the bottom of the casket like tokens,
return fare fallen to the pit
of a coat's satin pocket. (63–64)

This poem, written in blank verse, displays the speaker address-
ing the memory of her mother directly. She remembers how her
mother wanted to be buried in formal clothes, but also remembers
how her mother hated formality; she asks the memory of her mother
to remove the formal jewelry and go to the afterlife as she was in
life: plain, informal, unadorned. The eerie image of the gold becom-
ing fare to pay the ferryman to the afterlife—reminiscent of the old
custom of placing coins on the eyes of the deceased prior to burial
—becomes an image of love, perhaps a love the speaker and her
mother found difficult to express while the mother lived. That dual
tone of love and regret makes "The Fare" a powerful elegy for the
speaker's mother.

In *Original Love*, celebrations of love in the present lead to expressions of love in memorial, and those elegies lead to more fundamental questions about the nature of spiritual love in the third section—or, as Peacock titles it, "Another Love." This last section addresses questions of religious faith and love, a subject more difficult to address squarely than love of spouse or parent, which is a possible reason for the indefinite "another" in the title. "Forgiveness" is a characteristic example of this section's concerns:

> Forgiveness is not an abstraction for
> it needs a body to feel its relief.
> Knees, shoulders, spine are required to adore
> the lightness of a burden removed. Grief,
> like a journey over water completed,
> slides its keel in the packed sand reef.
> Forgiveness is contact with the belief
> that your only life must now be lived. Knees
> once sank into the leather of the pew with all
> the weight of created hell, of whom you did not ease,
> or what you did not seize. Now the shortfall
> that crippled your posture finds sudden peace
> in the muscular, physical brightness
> of a day alive: the felt lightness
> of existence self-created, forgiveness. (75)

This poem explores, with great precision, the actual lived sense of forgiveness—not as abstraction, but as actual experience. A variation of the sonnet form (15 lines instead of 14, rhymed ababcbbcd-cdceee), the poem draws a connection between the feeling of forgiveness and the feeling after a difficult journey: a feeling of ease and freedom. The striking image of the keel parked on the sand after long rowing conveys the theme. Forgiveness is an act of love for both the forgiver—who lifts the burden of shame—and the forgiven, once crippled, now muscular.

The sense of peace that "Forgiveness" portrays is hard-won, and serves as an emblem for the entire book: a sense of peace and serenity in self and love that all of Peacock's poetry has sought. In this sense, *Original Love* stands as a pivotal book in her career; it is her most focused collection, and contains some of her most powerful poetry—especially poems like "Little Miracle." The power, though, comes not from the denial of love (in all its aspects) but its achievement.

An interesting point about *Original Love* is that while the book represents a new turn for Peacock in tone and content, her approach to style remains the same as all her work since *Raw Heaven:* she bends various traditional forms to her colloquial, direct voice, sometimes loosening the forms in the service of a particular poem. In the past, Peacock has said that traditional form has allowed her to approach the charged subjects of her earlier poems. In *A Formal Feeling Comes,* an anthology of women's formal poetry, she writes:

> To me, formal verse makes impossible emotions possible. . . . It acts as a skeleton as well as a skin. It is a body. Verse form literally embodies the emotion of the poem, in the sense that embodiment both *is* and *contains* the life it is the body of. The need to embody the dangerous is both a need to surround it *and* then to live it. Therefore the initial choice is to contain and the subsequent writing allows the danger to live as made possible by the containment. (177–179)

In a recent interview, Peacock elaborates on this point. Drawing on a distinction that the critic Harold Schweitzer makes, she suggests that form allows her to "unbandage" painful experience in her poetry:

> If you take as a premise that all poems come from a wound, that there's an initial wound that sparks the poem—even if it's like a little nick or social slight—many poets have taken the initial wound and made of the poem a bandage for it so there's layer upon layer upon layer upon layer of bandaging, often so that the original wound or nick or slight is completely obscured to the reader, and perhaps was always obscured to the writer. Perhaps the writer never really understood why that poem got written, at the deepest psychological level.
>
> There's another kind of poem that is an *unbandaged* poem, where the writer is taking off bandages—psychological overlays, ignorance, denials, things that prevent the understanding of, the getting back

to, that original wound. I'm interested in that unbandaging experience. And that's why I'm not only a formal poet, but a personal poet, and I think that there's a thing called *personal poetry* in this country that suffers from a certain amount of pooh-poohing. (4)

In *Original Love,* the subjects of the poems have a different kind of emotional power—the bright rather than the dark side of love—than Peacock's earlier work, yet her skillful use of traditional form still enables her to convey that power. She has unbandaged self and love first to their pain, and now their joy. Any reader who has followed the emotional quest of Peacock's work will find a joyful resolution to her journey. That alone takes Peacock beyond the anguished Confessional tradition that influences her work, and brings her work into its own formal and narrative realm.

New Worlds: Frederick Turner

Among the Expansive poets, Frederick Turner (b. 1943) occupies a curious role. Turner is at once central and marginal, an enormously influential member of the group's inner circle and one whose work is virtually ignored. No one more self-consciously promotes—and exemplifies—the movement's main ideas and principles, and yet no one represents better the movement's persistent lack of recognition by the theoretical and poetic establishment.

Turner's centrality comes primarily through the way he has helped to promote the return to form and narrative. He first gained some attention in the late 1970s when, as a faculty member at Kenyon College, Turner re-established *The Kenyon Review.* During its heyday, the journal had been instrumental in establishing the New Criticism and poets associated with New Critical influence; under Turner's co-editorship with Ronald Sharp, the Expansive movement—not yet named as such—received some brief early attention with an issue in 1983. Another, more substantial source of Turner's reputation comes in his critical essays, which I discuss at greater length in chapter II.

Though Turner's work as a theorist is occasionally noted (usually by detractors of Expansive poetry, such as John Haines and Jonathan Holden, who cite "The Neural Lyre"), his poetry has attracted almost no notice. (An exception is his 1985 epic poem, *The New World*, attacked in detail by Thomas Byers and praised by Thomas M. Disch.) Few critics seem aware that Turner has published numerous books of poetry, a body of work impressive for its range—narrative, lyric and meditative, often blending the three modes in his longer science fiction poems—and skill. For the most part, Turner's poetry is simply ignored. Such a critical reaction is puzzling, given that within the history of poetry, the strongest critics are also practicing poets. This observation applies to major poets from Wordsworth and Coleridge to Adrienne Rich, and equally to influential critics whose poetry is not widely recognized, such as R.P. Blackmur and Yvor Winters. A recognition, however scant, of Turner's critical ideas about poetry should prompt critics to at least consider Turner's poetry, even if their judgment ultimately proves negative. (In fairness, many of Turner's books have been published in obscure small-press editions, rather than by university or New York presses. But such publication largely comprises the history of poetry; and such publication has not prevented other poets—such as the Language poets Bob Perelman and Charles Bernstein—from gaining wide recognition by critics.) But for whatever reason, if the meager discussion of Turner's work can be called a consensus, his reputation is as a polemicist for traditional aesthetics, and not much else.

To be sure, Turner's work as a theorist is significant. Turner's theoretical work shows the breadth of his interests—in science, in philosophy, in cultural history. From these diverse strands he has fashioned a coherent vision of humanity and the role of the arts and sciences in guiding humanity. And his poetry reflects the same interests. In fact, he has said that his poetry and essays are different modes of expressing the same ideas. Because of this, and given the originality of his theoretical ideas, an independent assessment of his poetry is difficult. Still, such an assessment is necessary and useful, because Turner's best work is a substantive contribution to the Expansive poetry school and to American poetry of the past three decades. This discussion will focus on two of his books: his 1985 epic, *The New World;* and a 1991 collection of shorter work, *April Wind and Other Poems.*

In a preface, Turner says *The New World* is intended "to demonstrate that a viable human future, a possible history, however imperfect, does lie beyond our present horizon of apparent cultural exhaustion and nuclear holocaust. Art has the world-saving function of imaginatively constructing other futures that do not involve the Götterdämmerung of mass suicide; because if there is no other imaginative future, we will surely indeed *choose* destruction, being as we are creatures of imagination" (vii). The poem depicts a post-apocalyptic United States in the year 2376. During this era, most of the world's natural resources have been depleted, and the old political, class and ethnic categories have been dissolved and re-defined. In *The New World,* the United States (now called "the Uess") is populated by four groups: the Burbs, descendants of the old middle classes; the Riots, violent descendants of the old inner-city slums, addicted to the neurochemical "joyjuice"; the Mad Counties, groups of fanatic religious fundamentalists; and the Free Counties, small Jeffersonian communities of democracy and culture.

The New World's narrative has several strands. Primarily it is a tale of family rivalry, focusing on two generations of the McClouds and the Quincys; this rivalry occurs against the backdrop of civil war in the post-apocalyptic United States. At the poem's beginning, the hero, James George Quincy, returns with his mother from Ahiah (Ohio) from exile in the region of Hattan Riot (Manhattan). Once in Ahiah, James encounters Shaker McCloud, patriarch of Mohican Free County; Shaker McCloud and James's father, George Quincy, had a falling-out years earlier, which was the source of James's earlier exile. James falls in love with Shaker's daughter Ruth and vows to make her his wife. He vows this despite the bad blood between Shaker and James, and despite the fact that Ruth has another suitor—Antony Manse, the county's military hero. Antony has saved Ruth from rape by Simon, her half-brother:

> Simon has moved behind her,
> and has sheltered her head with his arm, and has placed his other
>   hand
> flat on her navel, and smells the milky smell of her
> all afternoon cooped up, girl-flesh, clothes
> damp and wrinkled at creases and pleats. She moves
> away, and looks at his face, and at once she could die
> with the terror, his ugly mouth, the spots of pink
> on his cheek, the rage of terrible justice, the grief.
> He has touched with himself her buttock through the cloth
> and fate has determined the whole thing must be done.
> He moves on her, pleading; she catches herself, is bright,
> prosaic; and shuddering, chatters away to distract him;
> he with his dreadful strength rips the dress
> from her shoulders and bares the bird-wing clavicle,
> the flutter of plexus, the two pits of the hips;
> she does not know it, but cruelest of all, the egg
> in her loin, dispatch by the terrified organ's forlorn
> and immortal spasm, like the rich cluster of berries
> that burst out on the tree that is stricken, comes down
> as she fumbles with Kshatriya courage for the knife at her thigh.
> The blow grazes his ribs but he twists the blade
> from her hand, and the blood trickles over her ribcage
> and knee-tendon, ankle, and instep. He holds the knife
> to her throat, but she, with a jerk, tries to impale
> herself on it: he flings it away. But hooves, hooves!
> It is Antony Manse, he has leapt from his horse, in his arm
> the shawl she left at the house and that he is returning.
> He seizes Simon by the throat, and throws him aside. (69–70)

Ruth is devastated by this, and cannot muster physical desire for
James, even though he passes an arduous series of tests to become
her husband—tests that Antony, for all his physical and intellectual
skill, failed.

The conflict between Simon and James dominates the second
half of the book. Simon anoints himself the Messiah and leads an at-
tack on the Free Counties. After a long war, the Free Counties beat

back an all-out assault by the Mad Counties. However, the final assault is just a ploy to allow the Mad Counties to snatch James's son, Daniel. James knows that his feud with Simon will ultimately force him to fight Simon to the death: and yet if he dies, the loss to the Mohican County—whose hero he is—will be immeasurable. "He must betray his whole people, or his son" (165). Because he considers himself a man of honor, he consults with Kingfish—a sage who appears periodically in the poem to give James advice:

> "Ah give you one
> mo' gift, but ah ain't got no power
> any more to give it: permission." "Permission for what?"
> "Permission to break yo' own honor, man." (166)

James offers himself to Simon, unarmed, in exchange for Daniel. Simon agrees, but then at their meeting, James unsheathes his sword, which he had hidden: "'And thus,'/says James, 'I break my honor. Let no one speak/to me more'" (170). The result is a bloody confrontation:

> there
> before him, Simon, standing calmly, his sword
> drawn and a smile on his hurt and bitter lips.
> "Who wounds my flesh," he says, "is cursed, for upon his head
> lies the death of all my true disciples. My blood
> defiles my murderer and carries him down into Hell."
> "What do I care?" says James; "for I am a man
> who has lost his honor, and every curse you can utter
> slakes the thirst for pain that masters my life.
> Come on." They meet, strike, parry, as flames
> ripple and roar on the wall. But the rage of James
> George Quincy, Rollo the swordfinder, Jago
> the scourge of the dark crusade, Robin the eater
> of raw flesh, the wolf of the great snow,
> cannot be balked. For evil is capable only
> of evil; but good, being master of good, is master
> also of evil, and roused to evil is powerful
> far beyond the dreams of the evil. Do not

untie the knot of the good; for order and form,
like matter, are woven of energy bound to itself
so tight that the swiftness of knowledge, of light, must be bred
with itself to describe the fury pent in the grain.
And now the paneling burns, and the heat reddens
the faces of both of the brothers; Simon hews
at the waist of his enemy; James leaps in the air
and the blow passes beneath; Adamant whines
and through armor, flesh, and bone, the sword
of his father sinks to rest in the Messiah's side. (171)

Simon dies; James is himself killed by one of Simon's servants; and Ruth, in the end, marries Antony Manse, who had been her lover (with James's knowledge) all during her marriage; and the Uess enters a new period of peace.

Since *The New World*'s primary goal is to imagine an alternative universe, one of its major tasks thematically is to critique the present. It does so through a variety of means. One way is through the class structure that the poem depicts. The Free Counties, populated with renaissance men and women, represent Turner's highest ideal of humanity; he suggests (and his essays frequently argue) that our own age, with its intensive overspecialization by intellectuals, lacks a coherent vision necessary for the future of society. Similarly, the other classes—the Burbs, Riots and Mad Counties—represent the degeneration of those classes from the present to the future.

Of course, a more fundamental issue—of which the disintegrated classes are more a symptom than a cause—is our world's headlong rush toward destruction. As Turner notes in his preface, at the time of *The New World*'s writing, the Cold War—with its threat of nuclear Armageddon—still raged, and the poem depicts a world partially rebuilt from nuclear ruins. Significantly, *The New World* does not ask how such destruction can be avoided, but instead asks how humanity can survive such destruction.

In Turner's view, the chief way humanity can achieve such survival is through love, self-sacrifice and a concern for the world. These are the chief qualities of James George Quincy and Ruth McCloud.

Ruth loses sexual attraction for James because of the incident with Simon, but she still loves him, and then she makes love to him:

> And in three nights of consummate art she makes
> him believe he is loved and desired to the point of tears;
> and in his life of endurance and hope denied
> he has never known such happiness, lightness of heart,
>
> . . . .
>
> He has given to her, though she does not know it, a son;
> and it's all a noble pretense, a sacrifice, an act
> of supreme generosity. What is the truth in this world? (101)

Similarly, James sacrifices his honor—in some ways more precious to him than his own life—in attacking Simon, to save his son's life and avenge Ruth. Such quality is essential to leadership, Turner suggests. More fundamentally, such nobility—admittedly an idealized quality—is characteristic of the Free Counties' large vision, a vision that Turner argues is crucial to the future survival of humanity.

In the context of contemporary poetry, reading *The New World* is an unusual experience. Instead of adhering to twentieth-century epic structure, which is allusive and fragmented (i.e. *The Cantos, Paterson, The Changing Light at Sandover*), *The New World* re-invigorates traditional epic structure with its straightforward narrative, metrical line (a loose pentameter), and frequent philosophical digressions. The poem is not some Miltonic or Homeric throwback, however; its use of science fiction, a literary form from popular culture that has reached its zenith in the twentieth century, helps ensure that. More importantly, if some of the historical pressures that occasioned its writing (the Cold War and nuclear winter) have waned, others (class, ethnic and religious strife, the environmental crisis) have not. For its narrative context and technique, then, *The New World* demands attention. Its sheer scope (nearly 200 pages) allows for a deep and intricate exploration of contemporary concerns in a futuristic context. Turner develops an entire world, even a cosmology, in a way more reminiscent of huge novels like *Moby-Dick* than other twentieth-century long poems. (This reflects the fact that the novel has largely taken over the narrative functions that traditional epic poetry provided.)

That does not mean *The New World* is flawless. Its sheer scope makes its story uncompelling at times. The philosophic digressions, while necessary, also detract from the intensity that one usually expects of twentieth-century poetry. Because the poem has an argumentative, even didactic function, its ideas also invite disagreement. Some critics, focusing on the poem's class structure, fault the poem's vision as politically reactionary. In "Poetry and Politics," an essay in Robert McDowell's anthology *Poetry After Modernism*, Frederick Pollack argues, "In Frederick Turner the ethos of Reaganism has found its poetic voice" (23). And yet Turner hardly endorses the world he depicts; like all speculative fiction, *The New World* places contemporary historical currents onto the stage of the future.

Ultimately, *The New World* emerges as a unique and ambitious epic that succeeds where most twentieth-century epics do not: it offers a compelling narrative, philosophic depth, and most significantly, a distinctive, coherent cultural vision. By updating the traditional epic to contemporary concerns, *The New World* may ultimately stand as Turner's lasting achievement (though his 1988 epic about the terraforming of Mars, *Genesis,* is an underrated successor that offers a tauter narrative). Thomas Disch's summary in *The Castle of Indolence* is apt: "As a long narrative poem *The New World* has few equals in the English poetry of recent times, and as a work of science fiction there can be no doubt that it possesses an epochal significance. . . . This is a work of singular nobility and excellence; we must all be grateful to Turner for the love and labor that have gone into its creation" (104).

Because of the capaciousness of Turner's ideas, and his didactic impulse, his short poems are not always his best. His ideas require more space to develop deeply than the lyric allows. Turner's 1991 collection, *April Wind*, is best read as an extended meditative development of Turner's ideas, and the best poems are lyric sequences that delve more deeply than an individual short poem. A characteristic example is his sequence "First Base."

"First Base" is a poem about a traditional subject: a father's observation of his son's growth. Turner's treatment of the subject, however, is distinctive, since he fuses the subject with his perspectives about the relationship between the arts, sciences, and culture.

Part I begins the poem with an artistic invocation, to move from the present to the realm of art—to create art as the parents create a child:

> This ancient thing that must be done
> Requires the birth of one man's time,
> A prayer before it is begun,
> The island quiet of rhyme.
>
> Just as twelve years ago we fell
> To madness that begot a son
> And broke all caution in the spell
> Of conjugation,
>
> So now the fire must be set,
> The dishes put away, the door
> Locked fast that nothing hoarse might fret
> The birth of metaphor. (122)

In Part II, Turner observes his son on the baseball field, playing first base, and living a life independent from his parents. Such a life is compelled for children by both nature and culture—their biological growth and maturation, and the way their parents raise them. And such a life is both the joy and anguish of parents:

> Honor forbids my son to notice me,
> Setting his baseball cap against the glare.
> First baseman, he must watch the catcher's sign,
> Intimidate the batter with his stare
> Anchor the fielding into one design,
> And be the very animal and form
> Of his position in the baseball team,
> As bulls and meadowlarks fulfill the norm
> Designate for them by the chromosome.
> These cardinals, these cubs, these senators,
> How perfectly professional they seem,

Eleven-year-old gum-chewing matadors!
Wordsworth thought such a theater would come
Between the boy and his eternal home,
But what if we must all invent our being?
Is then the "master-light of all our seeing"
The actor's concentration on his part?
Then why this pain that brushes at my heart? (123)

Part III contrasts the world of Turner's birth with that of his son. Turner, son of the anthropologist Victor Turner, was born in England and grew up in Africa, where his father's work was based. Turner is now a naturalized American citizen whose son was born in the United States: "I am from Marx's Europe, the England of slums and the Beatles, / I am from Arthur's table, from the France of Cézanne and Courbet, / I am the last colonial, the sun went down on my childhood / In Northern Rhodesia, the drums rumbled all night and / My father read to me Shakespeare in the roar of the pressure lamp" (123). The world of Turner's birth is as different from his son's as can be:

And now what am I doing in Plano, Texas, on this hot after-
Noon in summer, the thunderclouds clear on the horizon like
Grotesque pieces of matte sunlit china, like
Stuffed toys to be given to baby dinosaurs, like the
Sound of a big rock band tuning up in a stadium?
What am I doing in Plano, with its malls and pyramids? (124)

Because of their differences, Turner notes in Part IV, his son must guide his father through his world:

My brave son Ben, watching the pitch come down,
Must teach impossible progenitors
How to be parents to a Texan child;
And over there in Warsaw, Budapest,
And East Berlin they wash the bloody hands
Of Beethoven and Sartre, and gently show
Their blood-drunk parents just how to be free.
All that I know of baseball comes from Ben.
How is it I am rooted now in him? (124)

Part V is an aside in which Turner asks if he is adequate to capture the spirit of his son. In Part VI, Turner confesses his own limitations as a poet, bequeathing the art to younger poets and resuming the role of father, observing his growing son with love and pride: "Happily, I pass my possessions on to them; now I prepare for my/ Metamorphosis into another being, smelling of/Evening, of thunderstorms over the horizon, of darkening grass" (126). Here is Part VII in its entirety:

> But soon the floodlights are turned on,
> As Plano tilts against the sky,
> And endless time piles up above
> The ballfield's little lighted octagon;
>
> An orange skin of evening glows
> Beneath the bluelit towers of cloud;
> A few drops fall, the game goes on;
> The warm, coyote-smelling wind still blows;
>
> The crackle of an utterance
> Above the curvature of pain
> Echoes in rumbles from the ground
> and holds the players in a moment's trance;
>
> The batter hits a loaded fly,
> Ben edges under it, elbows
> His baseball cap out of his eye,
> And takes it quickly, fires it home, as I
>
> Marvel how second nature grows
> Its subtle graft upon the first;
> And now another lightning burst
> Has turned the clouds into a purple rose. (126–127)

What is the "second nature" that Turner praises? It is the lives humans build for themselves, the way humans determine their own destiny, apart from animal instinct, or "human nature"—but which is, in Turner's view, the real human nature, the way humans operate both within and above nature. This complex idea about the intersections of nature and culture, expressed in a variety of verse forms, is at the heart of Turner's vision of humanity's role in the universe.

The poem's formal diversity—itself a kind of human invention reflective of nature's meaning—is part of the poem's content as well. For Turner, meter and rhyme function as a kind of "strange attractor" (a term from chaos theory to describe a simplicity around which complex patterns emerge), and meter and rhyme themselves are a subtext of the poem, functioning as a kind of theme (in their recurrence) and variation (in the different measures Turner uses—quatrains, blank verse, pentameter, tetrameter), allowing Turner to delve more deeply into his conventional subject. The poem's division into sections itself performs the coming into knowledge that is part of the poem's subject; the formal diversity plays a role in this as well. "First Base" stands as one of Turner's finest shorter poems.

Turner's best work establishes him as a poet of considerable achievement—one whose poetry features great intellectual sweep, narrative drive, and formal skill. His epics are singular. That his work has received so little attention, let alone the attention it deserves, is a serious critical oversight. Of course, any poet as prolific as Turner will be uneven. But his major work has earned him a place among the significant poets of the twentieth century—just as his critical work, also underrated, has earned him a place among the original theorists of the century. Turner is one of the essential Expansive poets.

5

Strumming the Lyre

Grosholz, Hadas, Steele

The lyric is traditionally the mode of poetry most associated with rhyme and meter. Poetry and song have a common ancestry, and rhyme and meter serve the same function in both: to add a musical element of both rhythm (the meter) and melody (rhyme). But as lyric poetry evolved from its roots in song—shedding its musical accompaniment—meter and rhyme came to serve other functions: intensity and memorability. And this had certain consequences. The musicality and brevity that rhyme and meter bring to the lyric make it more suitable for certain subjects—the treatment of a particular scene, emotion, idea or episode—and less suitable for others (lengthy stories, or complex philosophical issues—though extended sequences of lyrics can successfully address such issues).

In the twentieth century, dominated by the free verse revolution, poetry came increasingly to be identified with lyric—primarily because good free verse, lacking the rhythmic regularity of rhyme and meter, tended to make extensive use of other aspects of sound form to achieve intensity (assonance, consonance, alliteration) and, influenced by Modernism, concentrated on direct, unadorned presentation of images to portray its subjects. This led, in turn, to an increasing identification of poetry not only with lyric but with a narrow type of lyric free verse. Although poets continued to do distinguished work in traditional lyric forms—Elizabeth Bishop, Richard Wilbur, Anthony Hecht, Josephine Jacobsen—lyricism that made use of rhyme and meter remained the exception rather than the rule, particularly from the 1960s to the 1980s.

The three poets under discussion in this chapter—Emily Grosholz, Rachel Hadas, and Timothy Steele—all challenge the identification of lyric with free verse. Each works effectively in a variety of forms to address a number of contemporary subjects and themes. Grosholz is a poet of refined music and intelligence whose work asks how we as humans achieve connectedness with ourselves, with each other, with the larger world. Hadas is a poet most concerned with the flow of time; her poems, frequently elegiac, approach this subject from a wide range of perspectives. Finally, Steele is the most traditionally lyric poet, in the sense that he writes distinct poems rather than obsessively chasing one or two subjects; still, his work deals broadly and memorably with the intersections between nature and human nature.

The Music of Intellect: Emily Grosholz

Emily Grosholz (born 1950) is a poet of extreme refinement, both intellectual and aesthetic. Her poems are often philosophical in their aims—an unsurprising fact, given that Grosholz is a philosopher by profession (she teaches philosophy, rather than creative writing, at the university level). As well, her line is understated but undeniably formal in its music, seldom straying far from a pentameter foundation. She uses the lyric mode to ask larger questions about humanity —how do we achieve connectedness with others, with ourselves, with the world?—without sacrificing the musical richness and linguistic intensity that distinguishes lyric poetry from other modes of writing.

Grosholz has published three books: *The River Painter* (1984), *Shores and Headlands* (1988) and *Eden* (1992). In them, she treats a variety of subjects, including art, travel, and family. Rather than arranging her books as extended meditations on her subjects, she tends to organize clusters of poems around particular subjects, from which larger themes emerge. This discussion will focus on Grosholz's second and third books.

Shores and Headlands is a book about human relationships and place, the search for location. Many of the poems discuss travel—literal travel to far points of the world, or metaphoric travel through art and history—and the human search for connection. "Siesta" is a characteristic example of the book's themes, and of Grosholz's technique:

> All afternoon the heat intensifies
> in leaps, like goats climbing the terraced hills;
> another fig bursts on the tree; the olives
> surrender another cache of livid shadow.
> Cicadas transpose their note to a higher key.
> As if the ear were the most material sense,
> they sing us back to flesh and bone, the steep
> rocky quarter acre where we happen to live.
>
> But the eye is aethereal, that watches over
> the tranquil cool Aegean, mantle of blue
> woven east and west with the stitch of wind.
> We see beyond our country into another,
> familiar, never attained, where scattered islands
> gather like the dream's immortal children. (19)

Though "Siesta" is unrhymed, the poem nonetheless makes extensive use of the formal elements of sound. The octave describes a hot, languid afternoon, and Grosholz's lines embody the heat with their heavy consonance: "All afternoon the heat intensifies"; "goats climbing the terraced hills". The sestet, though, shifts the view from the rugged terrain to the open sea it overlooks, and Grosholz's line shifts from consonant to vowel: "the eye is aethereal, that watches over/the tranquil cool Aegean." The contrast between "the steep/

rocky quarter acre where we happen to live" and the sea, "familiar, never attained, where scattered islands/gather like the dream's immortal children," is striking. The poem is relatively straightforward in its images, but Grosholz notes her setting—Spendouri, Aegina—to indicate her cosmopolitan interests in exotic locales. The poem is one of a number of similar poems in *Shores and Headlands*, and is an accessible example of many of her characteristic traits.

"Theories of Vision" is a longer, more complex embodiment of *Shores and Headlands'* themes. Instead of focusing on a particular place in the world, the poem asks how we perceived the world. The poem is divided into five sections, each of which offers a different angle of perception on its subject.

Part One, written in an accentual trimeter line, contrasts an artist's rendering of the world with the actual world:

> Train the eye to see
> colors long faded
> from the marble throat
> of Immortality;
> colors past the sill
> of our red and purple,
> sheer embroidery
> on petals of the white
> violet, white rose.
>
> Train the hand to draw
> straight lines, circles
> true as the simple
> motions of the planets
> and elements that fall,
> so the empty brush
> above white paper
> traces to their source
> rivers of the air. (34)

The heart, Grosholz says, must learn a "certain renunciation" of the brush's rendering. The physical world, messy and infinitely complex, is both less and more than the artist's vision of it.

In the second part, written in a looser three-four beat accentual line, the speaker observes a peacock and has this realization about color:

> Destructive interference!
> Which, for a given thickness
> of film, only allows one color through.
> So, on the peacock's wing,
> here it is royal purple,
> there it is blue:
> quarrels of luminous children
> crossing, of space and time,
> the unending recess. (35)

That observation about color and light frequency is extended in the third section, written in iambic pentameter. The speaker observes a young girl blowing bubbles, "rainbows clasping their selvages at every corner":

> Rise, oh rise, she says, fantastic creatures,
> though even she must see the midsummer air
> is powerless to hold them, as the colors
> drown, all the invisible hands let go at once. (35)

Section Four, written in free verse, describes the physical and chemical processes that occur in the seeing eye:

> Visible light goes in
> the eye's black iris
> (flowing at the margin
> of a broad white river)
> and never comes out again.
> But absorbers are good emitters
> and black is best,
> so the eye also releases
> (fresh circles on the river)
> a different radiation
> invisible to itself, that runs beyond
> the roots of crimson, darker
> than wine, or blood. (35–36)

Part Five concludes the poem with a brief meditation on light itself, especially in sunrise and sunset. People measure their lives by light or dark, when they see and cannot see: "We lose each other every night/but dream of the recurrences/that unexpected morning brings." At night, prior to sleep, people settle together:

> So the scarlet voices chorus
> as the world begins to fall.
> Every longer evening brings us
> home to supper by the fire
> where the last light, slowly breaking,
> fans its rainbow on the wall. (36)

This is a satisfying conclusion to the poem.

"Theories of Vision" lives up to its title. It offers not one but many theories of how one perceives the world, and the significance of such perception. We perceive the world through the eye, as reflected light; we perceive the world and its light as rendered by the human hand on paper; we perceive the world through the effects of its light on our daily lives. The poem demonstrates Grosholz's lyric skill, philosophical inclination, and wide-ranging intellectual interests. It also mirrors, in its formal diversity, a large portion of *Shores and Headlands,* a book of lyric grace and intellectual depth.

One consequence of *Shores and Headlands'* sophistication is a certain impersonal tone, a tone of distance rather than intimacy. Grosholz's most recent book, *Eden,* is quite different in its tone. Without losing her musicality or intelligence, Grosholz explores subjects of daily human experience: memories of childhood and family; the different dimensions of love; the fears of parenthood. The poems explore the paradox between paradise and what can be realistically attained.

A significant theme in *Eden* is that of parenthood, a subject that Grosholz examines from dual perspectives: that of a daughter remembering her parents; and that of a mother observing her son. Parenthood is the crucial link between generations, as one is brought from the paradise of childhood to the knowledge of the adult world; one is guided in this way by one's parents, and one guides others as a parent.

One of the book's most powerful poems is "Life of a Salesman":

Behind the small, fixed windows of the album,
my father sits on sand, flowered with sea-salt,
nestling my younger brothers on his knees,
my mother beside him, me on another towel.

Or else he's smiling, lapped by shallow combers,
holding the kids so only their toes get wet,
free from booze and taxes, the city office,
his territory, miles of empty highway.

My husband, late addition to the family,
points out a disproportion: that generic
photo of my father on the beaches
stands for a man with two weeks' paid vacation.

I say to my brothers, look, you're all contented!
Both of you blue with cold in your ratty towels,
thrilled with the wind, the escalating waves,
our father watching the ocean roll its sevens.

Most of the time, he's on the road again
settling fancy letterhead, engravings
the businessmen he calls on can't be certain
they need, without his powers of persuasion.

He tries to tell them. Fifty weeks a year,
in sun and rain and snow, on secondary
arteries crosshatching the back country
of Pennsylvania, Maryland, West Virginia.

Alone at night in one more shabby diner,
his pale self in the speckled mirror-panels
is like a stranger's. He coats his potatoes
and minute-steak in catsup, for the color.

He wants a drink, but holds off for another
day, another hour. The gray Atlantic

shuffles invisibly. He orders coffee
and maybe calls his sponsor up, long distance.

Or calls my mother next, with lonely questions
she tries to answer, putting on my brothers
who sneeze and whistle, practice words like "daddy"
that touch him at the end of the conversation.

The dial tone doesn't sound at all like waves.
He might go to a movie, or a meeting:
there's always one around to fill the shady
dangerous intervals of middle evening.

He likes the coffee's warmth, the sound of voices
circling in on wisdom: know the difference.
Protect him, higher power, when he travels
his hundred miles tomorrow, rain or shine.

His death lies elsewhere, hidden in the future,
far away from his wife and children, far away
from cleanly riffled Jersey shores in summer,
the gray Atlantic playing out its hand. (38–40)

In this poem Grosholz recalls her father, who led the Willie
Loman lifestyle of a traveling salesman. She looks at her father's
image in a family photo, taken at the beach on a family vacation.
Her father was on the road the other fifty weeks of the year, selling
letterhead and similar products to businesses. It was a hardscrabble
way to make a middle-class living, but one her father did without
complaint. He would later meet a difficult death, but not at the
point the picture was taken. Though the picture spurs Grosholz's
memories, it is less notable for the family it depicts than the sym-
bolism her husband notes: it "stands for a man with two weeks' paid
vacation." It captured a moment of respite from a life not only of
hard work but of family separation; her father was mostly absent
from home, earning a living. The poem's concluding stanza, which
alludes to her father's death, extends this sense of separation.

The discovery of a parent's mortality, the limits of a parent's power, makes a child all too aware of her own limits. This is the perspective that informs the book's title poem, "Eden":

> In lurid cartoon colors, the big baby
> dinosaur steps backwards under the shadow
> of an approaching tyrannosaurus rex.
> "His mommy going to fix it," you remark,
> serenely anxious, hoping for the best.
>
> After the big explosion, after the lights
> go down inside the house and up the street,
> we rush outdoors to find a squirrel stopped
> in straws of half-gnawed cable. I explain,
> trying to fit the facts, "The squirrel is dead."
>
> No, you explain it otherwise to me.
> "He's sleeping. And his mommy going to come."
> Later, when the squirrel has been removed,
> "His mommy fix him," you insist, insisting
> on the right to know what you believe.
>
> The world is truly full of fabulous
> great and curious small inhabitants,
> and you're the freshly minted, unashamed
> Adam in this garden. You preside,
> appreciate, and judge our proper names.
>
> Like God, I brought you here.
> Like God, I seem to be omnipotent,
> mostly helpful, sometimes angry as hell.
> I fix whatever minor faults arise
> with bandaids, batteries, masking tape, and pills.
>
> But I am powerless, as you must know,
> to chase the serpent slicing in the grass,
> or the tall angel with the flaming sword
> who scares you when he rises suddenly
> behind the gates of sunset. (95–96)

Grosholz begins this poem, crisply written in blank verse, by noting her son's sure faith in a mother's ability to make everything right: "His mommy going to fix it." Her son is the "freshly minted, unashamed /Adam in this garden," and she is God, to him: "I seem to be omnipotent,/mostly helpful, sometimes angry as hell." But she knows she cannot protect him from his own fall, as her father could not protect her: they are all mortal, awaiting "the tall angel with the flaming sword." To Grosholz, one of a mother's duties is to inform her children of this fact: "But I am powerless, as you must know." This handing down of limitations, this deflation of Eden, binds one generation to the next. The poem, which concludes the book, makes this theme clear.

Although Grosholz works in a variety of forms, as this discussion has tried to show, iambic pentameter has exerted the most influence on her; she seldom strays far from an iambic base, even in her fluid free verse. She has written:

> In the decade after I turned sixteen, I covered a couple of meters of paper with poetic five finger exercises. . . . Without any reliable topics or firm experience, I nonetheless dimly felt that I was working on the "music" of my poems, and that establishing a music line was somehow essential to my project. . . . I was quite surprised to discover that what my ear had been unconsciously listening for all those years, and what my hand had finally learned how to produce, was iambic pentameter. But there it was, reams of it. (81)

Regardless of her subject, that "musical line" is present in all of Grosholz's poetry, and adds an undeniably lyric dimension to her intellectual explorations. The poems in *Shores and Headlands* seek human connection with the physical world; the poems of *Eden* locate human connection in generations, in family. Despite their somewhat different thematic focuses—and their highly different tones (one intellectual and reserved, the other colloquial and intimate), they collectively represent a deepening of this poet's core vision, and both demonstrate a graceful, musical lyricism. Grosholz's poetry, more than most, sings the music of the intellect.

The End of Time: Rachel Hadas

Rachel Hadas (born 1948) is a poet obsessed with time and its passages. Few write about the subject better than she. Over the past two decades, Hadas has published seven books of poetry, and nearly all of them deal with the subject of time in one way or another; taken together, they form a graceful and formal poetic map of the passage of time through human life, and of life's passage through time.

Over her seven books, Hadas's development has been steady. Hadas's early work is collected in *Starting from Troy* (1975), a short collection that explores varied subjects: the death of her father, the classicist Moses Hadas; poems of the Greek landscape, where Hadas lived for several years after graduating from college; and poems based on characters from classical myth. Hadas is already exploring her characteristic themes, but her distinctive style—poems in varied rhyme and metrical schemes, counterpointed with free verse—has not fully emerged. Hadas's second book is *Slow Transparency* (1983), a larger volume that more fully explores life in Greece, and concludes with a series of poems on a new marriage. Though *Slow Transparency* established her reputation, in this book Hadas is still developing her characteristic shape: many of the poems are crisp, lyric depictions of their subjects, but others strain for the appropriate balance between language and form. As a poet, Hadas has great philosophical inclinations, but those inclinations sometimes overwhelm her language. For instance, the concluding lines of "Marriage Rhapsody," the book's final poem, are anything but rhapsodic:

> Nothing is ever enough.
> Heavy water cautiously balanced in a pitcher
> spills on the flesh and sears it down to bone.
> Let the right blood have been broken in the test tube,
> the wrong blood solemnly recorded in a book of law,
> my flesh, my brand new bloodmate. If that's what makes a
> wedding,
> they rammed us into fact. No, we ourselves
> stood ringed with wishes. If that wasn't written

for us, let me have said
that as at the end of the fairytale
the marriage was accomplished.
But this is not the end. (88)

This tepid, prosy language is not the best way to conclude a volume of poetry, no matter how deep the intellectual exploration of the subject matter.

Hadas's poetry improved dramatically in her third volume, *A Son from Sleep* (1987), a short volume that recounts the subjects of pregnancy and birth. While many of the poems in *Slow Transparency* are slack or ponderous, most of the poems in *A Son from Sleep* are sharp and emotionally arresting, as these lines from "Two and One":

You weren't always here.
And you'll go. ("When?")
You'll disappear.
Birth / death: twin

mirrors reflecting
only each other
over the sleeping
head in the stroller

lose their power,
pale in one
brilliant hour
of living sun. (25)

These lines represent Hadas's great strength as a poet: wedding feeling with idea, the ear with the eye, in traditional forms. Generally, Hadas is a much better poet in traditional form than free verse, and these stanzas show why; they represent the pleasures of pure shape in their short dimeter lines.

Hadas continues to write about parenthood in *Pass It On* (1989), but extends her concerns to the broader issues of family across generations. This volume is perhaps her most accomplished one to date, both formally and intellectually. Her next two collections are *The Dream Machine* (1990; a long, blank verse poem to her son included in a volume of essays titled, characteristically, *Living in Time)* and *Mirrors of Astonishment* (1992), which continue Hadas's exploration of the relationships between time and life, and art's relation to them both. One difference between these books and her earlier ones is that they are more meditative than her earlier work, displaying an abstraction that her previous poetry did not. Hadas's latest book, *The Empty Bed* (1995), is a collection of elegies for friends and family who have died of cancer and of AIDS. This discussion will focus on Hadas's two best books, *Pass It On* and *The Empty Bed*.

In *Pass It On*, Hadas is concerned with the broad issue of family across generations. "Fix It (Winter)," a seven-part poem sequence, is a good example of the book's themes and of Hadas's formal technique. "Fix It" is primarily a series of poems about loss, death, and loneliness, written in a variety of forms. The poem elegizes the speaker's father, explores her relationship with a husband, and speculates about the future of her son, but sees no escape from the inevitable destination of life: death, loss. If life on earth itself is perpetual—at least in time as humans measure it, over millions and millions of years—each individual life ends, invariably.

The poem's first section, a variation of the Shakespearean sonnet (which unfolds its ideas through quatrains more dialectically than the octave-sestet Petrarchan sonnet), establishes the primary theme of loss, counterpointed with the understanding that life—in global terms—continues. "Heart's February: fill it in as bleak/and lonely," the speaker begins (15). But she notes immediately that she is about to give blood: "Picture a glacier bruising into bloom" (15). As her life-force literally drains from her, the speaker recognizes that her blood will mean life for someone else, but only provisionally—since that life will end too:

> I lie
> between two bodies, palming a red ball,
> flushed to pallor, gazing at the ceiling,
> as hollow days are damned into a crimson pool
> soon to be sealed and channeled to a stranger
> and even more precarious life. I'm filling
> a loving cup to raise to mortal danger. (15)

Danger, threats to life, are an inevitable part of life. The speaker's blood, a gift of life, also forebodes death.

The poem's second and third parts explore the speaker's relationship with her husband. In part two (written in blank verse) the speaker notes her connection with her husband one night, even though he has gotten up from bed to go in another room: "the beaded curtains stir://so I must sense, must pluck from winter air/the snatches of that song, or let the link//between our skulls (now stretched; now tighter) loosen./I shut my eyes and almost hear you think" (15-16). She chooses presence, however tentative, as a stay against absence; the blank verse subtly underscores the speaker's attempt to find continuity and presence. But that feeling is revised in the third section (another sonnet, this time Petrarchan), in which the speaker's husband is away, out of the house, and the speaker confronts the night alone. Her action: "Ineptly woo/some shabby cousin of oblivion/out of the garish hours after two" in a "ghost bedroom, chilly and too big" (16). Then, in the sestet, an abrupt memory of a precious necklace breaking:

> No, but the necklace! Burst
> and scattered agates sprayed apart and rolled
> under the furniture, and it was lost,
> the labyrinth of winter, overnight
> and not to be recovered. Somehow sealed
> in those cold globes was a whole summer's wealth of light. (16)

The necklace obviously has greater significance for the speaker than its material value; it conveys memories of summer, togetherness, a feeling that is lost to her now. There is no consolation in imagining presence; that consolation has been deflated by the memory (as well as presence) of loss.

In the next two parts, the speaker turns her attention to her relationship with her young son. In part four (written in rhyming quatrains), the son discovers imperfection in the world, what Hadas calls "the beautiful, the flawed/handiwork of God" (16). "*Broken!* he calls the moon/if it is less than round," the speaker notes (16). The son, though, finds his mother a reassuring presence, and thinks she can do anything: "His decree / *Fix it!* shows faith in me / that prompts me first to smile / / and then suppress a sigh / and fetching tape and glue / climb up to mend the blue / disasters in the sky" (17). Ultimately, all she can do is marvel at his innocence. The section ends by repeating its beginning stanza of short, pithy lines:

> I lean my ladder on
> the beautiful, the flawed
> handiwork of God
> and turn to spy my son. (17)

But her temporary consolation is again deflated by winter's oppressive reminders of loss. In part five, a villanelle—appropriate for its repeating phrases—focuses on the monotony of winter, not substantially relieved by motherhood. "It's not as if I'm lonely. I'm a mother, / busy with fixing—*pop* went that balloon" (17). The recurring phrases are variations of "deeper into winter" and "Agates roll downhill into the river"—here, the river is likely metaphoric, signifying "river of memory," since in part three the agates—with their connotations of light, warmth, and presence—rolled under furniture. Regardless, the speaker's outlook in this section is bleak: "What has been lost is gone and gone forever: / such knowledge is what forty winters mean" (17).

In part six, the poem's longest section, Hadas turns from traditional form to free verse; in the process, the speaker's rage at the monotony of loss comes forth. The speaker prepares to elegize her father, ferociously:

> Easier to instruct anyone else in the truth of feeling
>
> than to try to span the awful gap yourself,
> yourself to search for stones to leapfrog on
>
> across the—is it water or a tunnel?
> And in. And shut that door.
>
> . . . .
>
> Faces stuffed, we slam right out of this
> impossible world, propelled at speed

by terror, rage, loss,
and enter the shadow room of mourning. (18)

The "we" is the speaker and her son, and the person they come to mourn is her father: "not that the loss was fresh" (19). But in order to live her own life, however inevitably it will end, and to provide for her son's life, she must lay that loss in the past. Water, which fascinates her son, becomes an image both of past and future, the past frustrating even as it promises the future:

Subterranean fathers hollowly
boom at the bottom of their empty cistern

Drink me. My son's new interest in drains
and water fountains (mountains, as he calls them):

he squats or lies face down to peer below
the grating: stretches up to touch the water.

Mountain of water, shine another spring
so we can drink from you or wet our lips

or raise a chancy cup
and across the rim salute each other's

continued greenness. (19–20)

The speaker tells herself to find the agates scattered earlier and "restring them in another order" (21). The original order is not important to mourn; restring the necklace and go on living. That sense of loss of life and lives, even though it is omnipresent, cannot cripple what the living must do: live. That is the ultimate significance of the poem's title, "Fix It," and that significance is enhanced by the poem's seventh, thirteen-line section (a sonnet cut short). The son cries "Uppie, up!" (21), emblematic of growth. The speaker notes that "up" has other resonances as well, as in *shrivel up,* but then gives us an image of a shriveled plant: "Withered, a bush blows hard in autumn wind, / bald of petals now but still upright, / up, up, / obeying the commands of appetite" (21). An appetite for life ultimately devours the emotions of loss.

In this poem, Hadas writes in an unusual range of forms, which presents her meditations on living and loss in great complexity; each form is effective for the aspect of the theme it explores. The rhetorical rupture that the Petrarchan sonnet makes possible is appropriate for the sudden memory of the necklace in section three; the monotony of winter makes the villanelle in section five especially appropriate (more so than a sestina would be, where repetition becomes obsession, which would imply a paralysis by loss that the whole poem fights against); the fury of section six, where the speaker is too impatient to maintain a regular iambic beat (though some lines are regular), makes free verse an appropriate form. As a sequence, the poem's larger structure is open rather than closed, appropriate for its theme of the passage of life.

In *The Empty Bed*, Hadas not only memorializes people close to her—her mother, friends who have died of AIDS (Hadas has worked with gay health organizations)—but also examines the process of elegy itself, by which the living commemorate the dead to allow themselves to go on. This question is confronted directly in "The Friend," a long poem in rhyming couplets that concludes the book's first section. Hadas recalls an unnamed friend, apparently a fellow poet, who has recently died. This friend provided wonderful company when living, and also was a fellow poet who understood and stimulated Hadas's own writing: "all this time the thought of you / has been a part of what I do, / imagine, feel, especially write. / You stimulate each appetite" (21). Though poetry itself is a solitary pursuit, the company of other poets can help one—and of course poetry itself aims to connect one human being to another. In this respect, poetry—in one sense the most individual of pursuits—joins with love, the most social of pursuits. And, thus, elegy is an act of loving remembrance for one who dies, as the poem's closing lines make clear:

> And with September close at hand
> I have to heed this cold command
> and shut your lovely face away.
> With your mortality at bay

as if it were my own, I start
to raise a wall around my heart
in time for school, where every book
will render back your questioning look.
Behind each page I try to teach,
I'll sense you slipping out of reach.
Slowly, as in a dream of fear,
deeply familiar, deeply dear
friend, you drift, you float, you glide.
Stranded on the season's side,
I stare until my eyes are sore.
I stare till I can stare no more,
then turn to winter's lexicon
and try to write our friendship down. (22–23)

In these lines, Hadas enacts the process of memorialization through verse. Remembering her friend, she is nonetheless called back to her own life, and knows she will "sense you slipping out of reach." But out of memory, she will "try to write our friendship down": both proceeding with her own life as a poet, and preserving some part of his own. The poem establishes this preservation through elegant tetrameter couplets.

In another poem, "Upon My Mother's Death" (which supplies the book's evocative title with its image of "the empty bed"), Hadas elegizes her mother, and reflects on the conflicted emotions that accompany death:

The empty bed. And instantly I knew
and also didn't, as I do
and do not even now

where she had gone
precipitously, leaving me alone
to telephone

and do whatever else had to be done.
First, for example, furnish my ID
lest some impostor claiming to be me

should grab her few belongings; next, take them
in long sealed boxes home (but now whose home?);
and last myself continue to become

her who was gone.
This gradual process had been going on
for all our two lives' simultaneous span

but now I lifted her
once chunky person, feather-
light abruptly now, henceforth, forever,

ferried her backward from the empty bed.
Where? Anywhere instead
of that pristine dominion of the dead,

straight to the corridor
where chatting nurses eyed a visitor:
would this belated daughter shed a tear?

No. Yes. No. Yes. Then I absorbed the sense,
the respite, brief and sweet, the recompense
living, to love the quick and dead at once.

Deciphering this later, I read "lose"
for love—a logic I dare not refuse.
Love lorn live lose lone: need we really choose?

As when I wrote of C "Your absence walks"
but later read it as "Your absence works";
Both ways mean a blurry sleeper wakes.

Again, C, dying, left some books to me—
or was it "lent" them? Generosity
either way you read it—legacy

stretching across the boundaries of love,
defying the short time we're let to live,
the scanty sum it's possible to give.

Only for grief is our capacity
limitless. Illegibility
has a silver lining, I now see.

It blurs the limits of mortality.   (39–40)

This is a complex poem, one that confronts the emotional paradoxes of life and death. Hadas recounts how she tends to her mother's affairs after her death, and recognizes that she is continuing "to become//her who was gone," and recognizes where her mother has gone: once heavy, now light, "forever," in memory. The ambivalent emotion of whether to cry arises; she cannot decide. Then Hadas recalls other confusions, misreading "love" as "lose," and asking: "need we really choose?" The answer, of course, is no, because the two are intertwined. And the poem moves deftly over this intellectually and emotionally difficult question to a sharp observation: the confusion, the illegibility, "blurs the limits of mortality"; the very confusion associated with grieving over death can bring comfort, for it immerses one in living, obscuring the cold fact that all lives must end. This observation comes in one crisp line after several stanzas of rhymed iambic pentameter triplets, an effective formal construction that anchors the confusion in clear rhythm.

If Hadas's core subject—time—is one of the most traditional for a poet, and her use of rhyme and meter is also deeply rooted in tradition, her poetry is undeniably contemporary. The AIDS elegies in *The Empty Bed* touch on one of the central crises of our time. Her other poems about motherhood and childhood, while less engaged with politics, nonetheless engage common American experiences— the fears that parents and children face. Hadas is a poet whose achievement, while slowly evolving, is now rare: a formal *virtuosa* whose poems are also striking for their depiction of concerns that are at once contemporary and unchanging, fundamental to human experience.

Nature and Human Nature: Timothy Steele

Of all the Expansive poets, Timothy Steele (born 1948) is the most traditionally lyric—and the most traditionally formal. Some of his poems explore (presumably) the author's life; some are dramatic epilogues, and some are epigrams; still others are discursive investigations of abstract topics. But with the exception of a few poems in a loosely accentual line, none of them is in free verse. Perhaps no one more exemplifies the "traditional form" aspect of the Expansive movement than Steele.

Steele is traditional in several senses. First, he is traditional in his choice of forms: all three of his books are written exclusively in various metrical and rhyme schemes, and in a plain language that descends from Ben Jonson and John Dryden to Robert Frost and Yvor Winters in the twentieth century. Second, he is traditional in his approach to his subject: he presents his ideas and emotions directly, clearly, and logically, in a manner that can be easily paraphrased, usually without the indirection, allusiveness and irony that characterizes much contemporary poetry. And third, he is traditional in his method: he writes poems about a variety of subjects that engage his interest, and though larger themes can be discerned in his work, he does not obsessively chase one or two subjects, as do many contemporary poets. This discussion will focus on all three of Steele's books: *Uncertainties and Rest* (1979); *Sapphics Against Anger* (1986); and *The Color Wheel* (1994). (His first two books, slightly revised, were reissued in a single volume in 1995, the basis of the poems discussed here.)

Steele's poetry is best described by a statement he makes in his critical book, *Missing Measures: Modern Poetry and the Revolt Against Meter* (Arkansas, 1990):

> What is most essential to human life and to its continuance remains a love of nature, an enthusiasm for justice, a readiness of good humor, a spontaneous susceptibility to beauty and joy, an interest in our past, a hope for our future, and, above all, a desire that others should have the opportunity and encouragement to share in those qualities. An art of measured speech nourishes these qualities in a way no other pursuit can. (294)

Though Steele intended this as a general statement, it reveals much about his own poetry; Steele's poetry is frequently about nature, finds beauty and joy where others might overlook them, maintains a steady, calm tone, and depicts these concerns in clear language cast in traditional modes. In an interview, he used a concise phrase to sum up these observations: "Once when asked a question like this, I said my poems are about nature or human nature" (6).

Though Steele's first book is an accomplished one, its title suggests that *Uncertainties and Rest* is a young man's book; the poems wrestle with uncertainties and alienation, searching for rest and security. Several of the poems depict tones of alienation and despair, as does "Baker Beach at Sunset," revised when it was re-issued:

> ### July 4, 1976
>
> This is a place the ocean comes to die,
> A small beach backed by trashcans and concrete.
> Bits of torn paper scrape the sand; the sky
> Supports a few gulls. Words seem obsolete
>
> In settings such as these. The salt gusts blow
> The scent of marijuana up our way.
> No bathers in these tides, and, yes, I know
> I've written nothing in three months. Friends say
>
> That there's still gold in Modernist motifs—
> But I've learned what too much self-scrutiny
> Does to the spirit. Secondhand beliefs,
> The palpitating soul: how carefully
>
> We shelter and array these. Two jets fade
> West of the low sun, and the Golden Gate
> Shines with a kind of neo-gothic pride,
> A bright memorial of the welfare state.
>
> Seaward, tugboats and freighters lead and bear
> The commerce of the Far East and Marin;
> But gulls shriek at a distance, as if aware
> Of the grim age the tide is bringing in. (76)

In its form, this poem is characteristic of Steele's work: rhymed quatrains, an iambic pentameter line. Its world-weary, alienated tone —both blunt and obscure—is anomalous in Steele's body of work, and makes the poem a particularly interesting one in Steele's development in the way it confronts the issues of tradition, literary and otherwise. The poem's speaker walks a trashy beach alone, in despair, on the Bicentennial. Yet the poem does not turn to issues of American history, but the speaker's own sense of failure as a writer: "yes, I know / I've written nothing in three months." The speaker considers what his friends tell him—"there's still gold in those Modernist motifs"—but claims to reject them because of the corrosive effect of self-scrutiny on the spirit. The poem, though, is ambivalent about those "Modernist motifs." While it claims to reject them, it also exploits them: the poem is all mood and implicit idea, ending on a harsh note of despair while resolving little. Steele more typically works his poems to a clear conclusion, in which ideas rise cleanly from the scenes he depicts.

Another poem, "Last Night as You Slept," counterpoints the alienation of "Baker Beach at Sunset" with the sense of peace the collection seeks:

> The clock's dial a luminous two-ten,
> Its faint glow on pillow and sheet,
> I woke—and the good fatigue and heat
> We'd shared were gone; and I, sensing again
>
> Distance as chill as the light on the shades,
> Was so uncertain, love, of our rest
> That I woke you almost as I drew my chest
> Against the warm wings of your shoulder blades.
> (79)

This poem is more characteristic of Steele's work in its tone—the intimacy that is so essential to love poems (and Steele is an outstanding love poet)—and in the way it finds great resonance in a simple, everyday scene, without straining language to assert the resonance. Although "Last Night as You Slept" is a simple poem, its gracefulness is not a simple achievement.

During the seven years between *Uncertainties and Rest* and *Sapphics Against Anger*, Steele's work underwent a subtle maturation. As noted, he was already accomplished formally when his first book was published, but he left behind the youthful alienation that was so prevalent in *Uncertainties and Rest*. In fact, *Sapphics Against Anger*, to a degree, critiques the restless passion of the poems in the earlier book. The collection's title poem is a case in point:

> Angered, may I be near a glass of water;
> May my first impulse be to think of Silence,
> Its deities (who are they? do, in fact, they
> Exist? etc.).
>
> May I recall what Aristotle says of
> The subject: to give vent to rage is not to
> Release it but to be increasingly prone
> To its incursions.
>
> May I imagine being in the *Inferno*,
> Hearing it asked: "Virgilio mio, who's
> That sulking with Achilles there?" and hearing
> Virgil say: "Dante,
>
> That fellow, at the slightest provocation
> Slammed phone receivers down, and waved his arms like
> A madman. What Atilla did to Europe,
> What Genghis Khan did
>
> To Asia, that poor dope did to his marriage."
> May I, that is, put learning to good purpose,
> Mindful that melancholy is a sin, though
> Stylish at present.
>
> Better than rage is the post-dinner quiet,
> The sink's warm turbulence, the streaming platters,
> The suds rehearsing down the drain in spirals
> In the last rinsing.
>
> For what is, after all, the good life save that
> Conducted thoughtfully, and what is passion
> If not the holiest of powers, sustaining
> Only if mastered. (12)

In his important early essay on Expansive poetry, "Reading the New Formalists," Robert McPhillips speaks of Steele's "distinctly neoclassic sensibility which enables him to write clearly on any number of subjects" (311–312). "Sapphics Against Anger" is a particularly good example of that sensibility at work. Steele uses a classical Greek form, the sapphic (organized by syllable count), and a classical poetic mode, the verse essay, to address a subject at once contemporary and ancient: anger and its effects on human relationships. Like a prose essay, the poem addresses the abstract idea of anger, bringing in specific examples to support its points (though it does so more lyrically than a prose essay, as in the graceful image of "the suds rehearsing down the drain in spirals / In the last rinsing); Steele argues that anger, needlessly vented, can destroy relationships, and that the passion that fuels anger is "sustaining / Only if mastered." The poem's rueful assertion that "melancholy is a sin, though / Stylish at present" represents the shift in Steele's work from his first book to his second.

Perhaps the strongest poem in *Sapphics Against Anger* is "Near Olympic," a long exploration of a mixed west Los Angeles neighborhood. Written in rhymed couplets, Steele's portrait of that landscape and the people who inhabit it is affectionate and detailed, bristling with observation:

> The neighborhood, part Japanese and part
> Chicano, wears its poverty like art
> Exotic in its motley oddities.
> Over dirt driveways hang banana trees;
> In front of small square stucco houses bloom
> Broad jacarandas whose rain-washed perfume
> At morning half redeems the rush-hour released
> Swelled roaring off the freeway six blocks east.
> Along the street sit Fords and Oldsmobiles,
> Lowslung and ancient; or—with raised rear wheels
> And sides flame-painted—Mustangs and Chevelles.
> And in the courtyards of one-time motels
> In which the poorer families live, there grow

Sweet corn and yellow squash, and chickens go
Jerkily here and there, loud squawkings borne
Through limp, arched iris leaves and stalks of corn. (20)

Most would likely describe this as a junky, impoverished land-
scape, but Steele finds surprising beauty in the mixture of human
relics and struggling nature: car exhaust and jacaranda scents;
rusted-out cars and gardens with livestock. The two are enmeshed
in that particular place, giving it its distinctive character: a place in
which survival, though a constant struggle, is achieved, and some-
times something greater than mere survival emerges. That charac-
ter is also manifested in the people who live in the neighborhood, as
Steele demonstrates:

This is the hour of casual casualties.
Birds clatter in the stiff fronds of palm trees,
The bustle that the twilight's always fed.
The mother strokes her daughter's jet black head;
The child makes choppy trooper steps toward the walk.
Some older children bike along the block,
A girl there crying, *No one catches me,*
Glancing back quickly, pumping furiously
Off from the others. Bent to handlebars,
Only one boy pursues her. Past parked cars,
It's *No one catches me,* and nearly night.
No eyes are following the girl's delight—
At least not Carlos's or the young mother's.
Nor do their eyes meet, ever, one another's.
It is as if they do not see or hear.
The mother will be nineteen come next year,
And Carlos twenty. What they are survives
The limpid vacancies of air, their lives
Now like some urgent, unobtrusive thing,
Withdrawn and lovely and diminishing. (15–16)

The young girl who rides her bike and screams, *"No one catches
me!"*, is filled with spirit, and has not yet met the defeat that others

of the neighborhood have encountered, such as the father and mother; not even 20, both are already grim and pessimistic, not even able to share joy in raising their daughter. Perhaps they know better than the girl who thinks no one will catch her; they have been caught. Yet the small beauties that persist in the neighborhood—the jacaranda scents, the "limpid vacancies of air," the young girl's fearlessness—do not seem entirely threatened, even as they are "withdrawn and lovely and diminishing." Steele finds some hope in the scene that survival will continue, however difficult that may be.

"Near Olympic" brings together two significant tendencies in Steele's work: observation of the natural world and of human character. His interest in both has been apparent from the start, but he has deepened his vision with each successive book, even as his tone has settled: "He is particularly even-tempered on all occasions," McPhillips writes (314). That deepening is clearly evident in his most recent book, *The Color Wheel*. "Portrait of the Artist as a Young Child" is a good example:

> Your favorite crayon is Midnight Blue
> (Hurrah for dark dramatic skies!)
> Though inwardly it makes you drone
> To see it like an ice-cream cone
> Shrink with too zealous exercise.
>
> But soon you're offering for review
> Sheets where Magenta flowers blaze.
> And here's a field whose mass and weight
> Incontrovertibly indicate
> You're in your Burnt Sienna phase.
>
> Long may you study color, pore
> Over Maroon, Peach, Pine Green, Teal.
> I think of my astonishment
> When first I saw the spectrum bent
> Around into a color wheel,
>
> A disc of white there at the core,
> The outer colors vivid, wild.
> Red, with its long wavelengths, met

With much-refracted violet,
And all with all were reconciled.

When I look past you now, I see
The winter amaryllis bloom
Above its terra-cotta pot
Whose earthen orange-apricot
Lends warmth to the entire room.

And cherry and mahogany
Introduce tones of brown and plum;
While by the hearth a basket holds
Balls of yarn—purples, greens and golds
That you may wear in years to come.

Yet for the moment you dispense
Color yourself. Again you kneel:
Your left hand spread out, holding still
The paper you'll with fervor fill,
You're off and traveling through the wheel

Of contrasts and of complements,
Where every shade divides and blends,
Where you find those that you prefer,
Where being is not linear,
But bright and deep, and never ends. (32–33)

In this poem, Steele combines nature and human nature through a close observation of a child's first experience with crayons. The poem depicts the child's wonder in re-creating the world's color with crayons, and the speaker recalls his own experience at seeing an actual color wheel—a beam of light broken into its full spectrum of visible color. In a spectrum of light, each band of color modulates inseparably into the next, and neat divisions are impossible; all are interconnected. Turning his attention back to the present, the speaker sees similar connections between colors in the child's room, and connects the child's wonder to that interconnectedness: "Where being is not linear/But bright and deep, and never ends." It is a precious place, too easily lost.

"December in Los Angeles" is another example of how Steele

observes the intersections of nature and human nature, and also exemplifies the shift in his perspective that has occurred since his earliest book:

> The tulip bulbs rest darkly in the fridge
> To get the winter they can't get outside;
> The drought and warm winds alter and abridge
> The season till it almost seems denied.
>
> A bright road-running scrub jay plies his bill,
> While searching through the garden like a sleuth
> For peanuts that he's buried in the soil:
> How different from the winters of my youth.
>
> Back in Vermont, we'd dress on furnace vents.
> A breakfast of hot cereal—and then
> We'd forge out to a climate so intense
> It would have daunted Scott and Amundsen.
>
> I'd race down icy Howard Street to catch
> The school bus and pursue it, as it roared
> Up Union, my arms waving, pleading, much
> To the amusement of my friends on board.
>
> But here I look out on a garden, whose
> Poor flowers are knocked over on their side.
> Well, stakes and ties will cure them of the blues
> (If not the winds) and see them rectified.
>
> And in the shower is a pail we use
> To catch and save the water while it warms:
> I fetch and pour it on the irises
> And hope this winter will bring drenching storms. (52–53)

This poem notes the contrast between the adult speaker's present balmy winter and the chilly winters of his youth. The speaker recalls his racing to catch the school bus on an icy street with amusement and affection, yet without undue nostalgia; he treats his present environment, Los Angeles, with as much tenderness as he does the past, hoping to bring forth beauty in the flowers. In this poem, observation of the natural environment blends with memory to paint a warm picture of human interaction with place.

Steele's critical ideas about traditional form and free verse, discussed at greatest length in *Missing Measures,* have exerted considerable influence on contemporary poetry. (I discuss *Missing Measures* in more depth in Chapter II.) But his own poetry, consistently graceful and fluid in its use of rhyme and meter, is perhaps his best argument in favor of those modes. Steele's poetry presents people searching for beauty and goodness in a difficult world. In his poems, they find what they seek—if only briefly. That is the essence of lyric poetry.

6

The Sword of Wit

Disch, Feirstein, Gwynn, Martin

The dominant position of the lyric in twentieth-century American poetry is clearly illustrated by the degree to which other poetic modes make use of lyric elements. The American epic is mostly comprised of lyric fragments knitted together, as in Pound or Williams. To the extent that narrative survives in the autobiographical poetry so prevalent since 1950, it does so chiefly through the lyrical anecdote or episode. Poets who are able to build extended sequences of such poems, such as Rita Dove in *Thomas and Beulah*, are hailed for their innovations in narrative. The question of whether the dominance of lyricism is good or bad is not to be decided here (though there is little doubt that this tradition has produced much beautiful poetry), but it is clear that many traditions have been marginalized by the lyric.

One such tradition is the satiric exploration of ideas about human culture, in which the poet mocks or attacks the vices and ills of human society. In the seventeenth and eighteenth centuries, poets such as Pope and Dryden wrote effortlessly, in serious and satiric modes, in crisp forms, about the pressing intellectual issues of their day. Like skillful essayists, their wit and ease of manner belied the depth and substance of their ideas.

In the twentieth century, W.H. Auden had some notable achievements in this mode, but few American poets have been able to assimilate his example without lapsing into mere imitation. Beyond Auden, a list of successful (not to say influential) American satiric poets is short indeed: X.J. Kennedy; J.V. Cunningham; Howard Nemerov; some of W.D. Snodgrass's recent work. The brevity of this list indicates how unfashionable the satiric mode has been in the twentieth century, when indirection, private vision, the image, and free verse have been dominant. This is the opposite of the satiric mode's features: direct statement, public discourse, the idea, and rhyme and meter.

One of the most striking—and unanticipated—achievements of Expansive poetry is the way it has revived the tradition of satiric, discursive poetry. Each of the four poets under discussion in this chapter work with considerable success in this mode. Thomas Disch writes in serious and light verse to mock a variety of dimensions of human society. Frederick Feirstein writes exceptional dramatic sequences that satirize our individual and collective tendency to forget our history. R.S. Gwynn relentlessly satirizes all aspects of human experience, both high and low. And Charles Martin deeply explores the complex ironies of politics and human history.

The Dark and the Light: Thomas Disch

Reviewing one of Thomas Disch's (born 1940) early books, Dana Gioia argues that one could virtually use Disch's work "to define the current mainstream of contemporary poetry dialectically through its opposites, so consistently antithetical is its approach from contemporary practice" (194). Gioia elaborates on Disch's strengths:

> Disch is concerned primarily with ideas not emotions (the free play of ideas, that is, not any particular ideology). His subjects are rarely personal, except insofar as Disch represents himself as what Auden once called "the average thinking man." He therefore cultivates a

general rather than a private voice. His tone is cosmopolitan and public rather than intimate and sincere. The structure of his poem more often depends on the logical progression of his ideas than on the associational links of his images. His natural manner is witty and discursive, not serious and lyrical. Most of his poems fall into traditional forms and genres, not the preferred nonce forms of contemporary poetics (when he does adopt the forms of contemporary poetry, it is almost always for parody). (194)

As an overview of Disch's best work, Gioia's observations ring true. More than most contemporary poets, Disch combines the discursive mode with a crisp formalism. Some of his best poems combine urbanity with gentle satire, as in his "Poems," his response to Joyce Kilmer's famous doggerel about trees:

> I think that I shall never read
> A tree of any shape or breed—
> For all its xylem and its phloem—
> As fascinating as a poem.
> Trees must make themselves and so
> They tend to seem a little slow
> To those accustomed to the pace
> Of poems that spread through time and space
> As fast as thought. We shouldn't blame
> The trees, of course; we'd be the same
> If we had roots instead of brains.
> While trees just grow, a poem explains,
> By precept and example, how
> Leaves develop on the bough
> And new ideas in the mind.
> A sensibility refined
> By reading many poems will be
> More able to admire a tree
> Than lumberjacks and nesting birds
> Who lack a poet's way with words
> And tend to look at any tree
> In terms of its utility.
> And so before we give our praise

> To pines and oaks and laurels and bays,
> We ought to celebrate the poems
> That made our human hearts their homes. (73)

In this poem the satire is gentle, the ironies understated, the intellectual reference worn lightly, and the form fluid. In short, it has all the virtues of a good informal essay. It demonstrates curiosity and humor in its ideas, and seems effortless in its mode of expression. Few contemporary poets demonstrate this particular kind of grace, or even aspire to do so.

Disch's American reputation as a poet is based primarily on *Yes, Let's* (1989), a volume of new and selected work, and *Dark Verses and Light* (1991). Prior to *Yes, Let's*, his work appeared almost exclusively in obscure small-press editions, mostly with English publishers, and he had little recognition as a poet (though he has published numerous genre novels). While Gioia's observations of Disch's best work are accurate, *Yes, Let's* also shows a poet of wider range—though not necessarily skill—than Gioia allows. In fact, some of Disch's poems directly contradict this remark of Gioia's: "Disch is every bit at one with his age as John Dryden would be in a surrealist café" (194). "To Jean-Ann" is characteristic:

> There is no use
> falling in love
> with the president of U.S. Rubber.
> Believe me.
>
> If I were my own mother,
> or, rather,
> if you were my son,
> I couldn't tell you any better.
>
> For your own good, Jean-Ann,
> for your own
> good, leave the president of U.
> S. Rubber alone. (35)

This poem, slack and gnomic, is at home only in a surrealist cafe; there seems to be no irony in these lines.

At some point during his development, though, Disch turned toward traditional forms and discursive modes, and the result is a poem such as "Entropic Villanelle" from the new poems in *Yes, Let's:*

> Things break down in different ways.
> > The odds say croupiers will win.
> We can't, for that, omit their praise.
>
> I have had heartburn several days,
> > And it's ten years since I've been thin.
> Things break down in different ways.
>
> Green is the lea and smooth as baise
> > Where witless sheep crop jessamine
> (We can't, for that, omit their praise),
>
> And meanwhile melanomas graze
> > Upon the meadows of the skin.
> (Things break down in different ways.)
>
> Though apples spoil, and meat decays,
> > And teeth erode like aspirin,
> We can't, for that, omit their praise.
>
> The odds still favor croupiers,
> > But give the wheel another spin.
> Things break down in different ways.
> We can't, for that, omit their praise. (29)

This is a superb poem. The villanelle is an especially appropriate form to explore the theme of entropy, or the slow dissipation of the universe's energy. The poem's repeating lines and images slowly wind themselves down to closure, embodying the varied processes of breakdown, and yet we still must pay attention to the things of the world, even as they decay. The poem is an elegant exploration of this theme.

Disch consolidates his achievements in this vein in his most recent book, *Dark Verses and Light,* a large gathering of new work. The book demonstrates his impressive facility with form and tone by living up to its title; the poems are variously dark and light, but also make use of tonal variety. Even the most humorous poems have an edge to them, and the darker poems are leavened by humor. One such poem is "The Friends of Long Ago," remorseless in its cruelty:

> Unwelcome guests come earliest.
> They linger in the kitchen, hungry
> For confidences. Their glasses
> Unerringly light on the best wood.
> Shameless as the wine they bring,
> They praise the food their presence turns
> To carrion. Their kisses are carcinogens.
> Only the eyes, trapped in their rims,
> Bear witness to the appetites and lies
> Once so ungrudgingly shared.
> Be resolute—ask after their torments—
> The novel abandoned, the ex-wife, the diet.
> When at last they leave, do not
> Let them forget their umbrellas. (40)

In Disch's view, these friends—who long ago wore out their welcome—are obnoxious, and deserve to be treated with scorn. "Ask after their torments"—a question especially designed to induce irritation, if not pain. The poem alludes to the decency these friends once displayed, but the poem asks no quarter in the present—and gives none.

A more complex poem is "The Snake in the Manger: A Christmas Legend." The poem blends humor—its form is a bumptious iambic tetrameter quatrain, with rhyming couplets—and seriousness, trying to fashion a parable combining the story of Genesis and the birth of Christ: the introduction of sin and goodness.

The poem begins with a conventional manger scene: the angels come to herald the birth of Christ. The animals of this Christmas story, however, are as intelligent as humans, and soon talk among themselves about how to welcome this event:

> A rooster crowed, as for the sun,
> "Now listen to me, everyone!
> I know now why we're in Judea.
> These wise men have the right idea.

> "*We* cannot give what's bought and sold—
> No myrrh or frankincense or gold—
> But we can give from what we've got—
> Even our little may help a lot."
>
> The cows looked grave, the sheep thought hard,
> And the chickens fluttered about the yard,
> As each considered what to bring
> As a suitable gift for the Manger's King. (4–5)

The animals are quite creative in thinking of gifts and gestures to make to the baby Jesus. At one point, they decide to present a variety show. "So back to the manger the animals filed / To present their show to the sleepy Child" (7).

The serpent, though, cannot decide what gift to bring. At first he brings a pelican's egg, larger than most eggs and more beautiful. Yet, lacking limbs, the snake can only carry the egg in its mouth, which does not work. "For while the snake had stopped and rested / The pelican's egg had been digested, / And all it could give was the broken shell. / 'God send,' it hissed, 'all fowl to Hell!'" (6). Instead, the snake tries to bring a hollow gourd to Jesus, but the gourd meets the same fate as the egg: he has swallowed it. Livid, the serpent prepares to give Jesus the one gift he has left—his fangs:

> Its disappointment turned to rage,
> And serpent nature took center stage.
> "If I can't achieve another thing,
> There's one surprise I still can spring."
>
> It coiled itself into a knot of spite.
> "Let *this* help you to sleep tonight
> Beneath the cold snow's deepest drift!"
> And it spread its jaws to give its Gift. (10)

But the snake, in its fury, twitches his tail—with the rattling gourd inside. This both alerts and delights Jesus. Jesus says (remember, this is a parable) the gift is "something to suit a baby's whims / Better than a hundred hymns" (10).

And the poem concludes:

> The serpent's tongue met the infant's lips
> Like the first taste of potato chips,
>
> And the child knew Sin, and the snake knew Love,
> And in the heavens high above
> The angels sang of Peace on Earth
> And the wonder of the God-Child's birth. (11)

The poem's nursery rhyme meter and comic tone give it the qualities of light verse on the surface. But unlike most light verse, "The Snake in the Manger" has deeper, more serious aims than comic effect. First, as an allegory about the creation of the rattlesnake and the introduction of goodness and sin, the poem is effective. Disch presents his story with great deftness, and its underlying theme is clear: goodness can redeem the evil tendencies in anyone. The snake, about to kill Jesus, is met with Jesus's love, and his good nature emerges. The poem effectively combines elements of the Christmas story and the Book of Genesis into a new comic parable. If the poem's view of human nature is idealistic, it is not naive; it acknowledges that circumstances may thwart good intentions, and bring about potential violence; and that good can calm such potential. By exploring such a theme, the poem challenges the reader's assumptions about light verse.

A more ambitious sequence in *Dark Verses and Light* is "The Joycelin Shrager Poems." Joycelin is a former underground filmmaker, now a poet. Her guiding aesthetic is spontaneity and the exploration of her life, craft be damned. In this respect, she is part and parcel of the counterculture, with its "anything goes, man" attitude toward aesthetics. Disch prefaces the poem with two prose selections, "The Joycelin Shrager Story," and a faux critical introduction by Joycelin's workshop instructor. "The Joycelin Shrager Story" is a short story, narrating in great deal her career as an underground filmmaker; the second selection is spoken by the voice of Andy Lowe, a leading teacher of creative writing. Lowe praises Shrager— the "guiding lite of moonchild press" as well as a budding poet—

and recalls with enthusiasm when she wrote her breakthrough poem, "i am just a plain poet":

> Rite from the nite of that April 1st class I could see that Joycelin had the one great essential for poetic success. She had a faith in herself that nothing could challenge, & because she did, we can too. (79)

One poem, "my assignment this week is a sonnet," bears out Lowe's observations:

> my assignment this week is a sonnet
> fortunately it doesn't have to rime
> as long as it has exactly 14 lines
> it'll be ok my teacher andy lowe
> who edits dial-tone in addition to
> teaching says he honestly wants to
> vomit when he sees rimes in a modern
> poet tho there is no one who respects
> the great traditions of english poetry
> more than andy take yr daily life
> andy says & put it under the microscope
> of poetry write a kind of newsletter
> about yr inner secrets and yr friends
> & if you've got more to say than
> there's room for in 14 lines or not
> enough don't worry the basic unit
> of modern poetry is the human breath divine (95)

Disch's poker-faced rendition not only of this seventeen-line sonnet but of the elaborate apparatus surrounding it—Joycelin's life story and the annotations of her work by her mentor, Andy—are the key to the poem's satire. This poem's deadpan rehearsal of every bad cliché of beat-derived poetry is hilarious; the poem's language and linebreaks are particularly reminiscent of Lyn Lifshin (except Lifshin has never attempted a formal poem). Disch mocks an entire subculture and its assumptions about art. Although the poems themselves would be an effective satire, the prose prefaces add depth and detail to Joycelin Shrager as a (pathetic) human being and artist—which makes Disch's satire all the richer.

Disch is not a poet of uniform achievement, but his best work shows a range of tone and formal skill unusual in contemporary poetry. He is an accomplished satirist and humorist, but can explore serious subjects with equal skill and finesse; he frequently works in both modes at once. And while he can work skillfully in free verse (more often than not to mock it), his greater accomplishment is the ease and variety of his traditional measures. He is a poet of urbanity and wit, traits that his criticism, collected in *The Castle of Indolence,* also displays. It took time for Disch's reputation to come close to his achievement; like other poets of his generation, such as Ted Kooser, he needed an early, mid-career new and selected poems to simply announce his excellence to a larger audience than the tiny circle of admirers who had sustained his early reputation. But as *Dark Verses and Light* demonstrates, Disch is now in the prime of his work.

Inner and Outer Drama: Frederick Feirstein

Among the Expansive poets, Frederick Feirstein's (born 1940) work may be among the most expansive—in the general sense of that term. His work combines a satirist's worldly eye, a consistent formalism, and a dramatic impulse that seeks out larger forms and sequences. Though his poetry is more notable for its ideas and stories than its formal qualities—Feirstein's work does not dazzle with its musicality—his work's mixture of narrative and discursive elements is singular within the school. His use of the sequence allows him to delve more deeply into his subjects than most poets, and also allows his work to accommodate a wide range of styles, forms and tones.

Feirstein has published seven books: *Survivors* (1975), *Manhattan Carnival* (1981), *Fathering* (1982), *Family History* (1986), *City Life* (1991), *Ending the Twentieth Century* (1995), and *New and Selected Poems* (1998). All feature extended narrative and dramatic sequences that take a sharp look, variously comic and sober, at contemporary culture. This discussion will focus on his two most recent books, *City Life* and *Ending the Twentieth Century,* which contain some of his strongest and most representative work.

City Life is divided into two sequences, "Larry's Neighborhood" and "The Psychiatrist at the Cocktail Party." The latter is the more interesting, and more complex, of the two. Spoken in the voices of numerous characters, "The Psychiatrist at the Cocktail Party" is a comic soap opera that explores several themes: the troubled relationships of Larry and his fiancée Joyce, and Renee and her husband Meato; the Republican radical chic of Latin American rebellion (the party's guest of honor is the rebel leader of Quistador, a fictional country); and the wry perspective of Ben Struthers, the psychiatrist whose point of view provides the narrative's anchor. The iambic poems, written in a variety of rhyming schemes, shift through a multitude of voices—some are addressed to the psychiatrist, others are spoken by him, and others provide additional perspective and narrative elements.

If the psychiatrist provides the anchoring perspective, the sequence's action revolves around Larry, the host of the cocktail party. This becomes evident in the sequence's opening poem, "Larry Corners the Psychiatrist." In short order, Larry confesses he is having second thoughts about marrying Joyce; that he has an oedipal fascination with women, alternately turned on and repulsed by what he perceives as their resemblance to his mother; and his emerging attraction to Renee, an old college friend married to the wealthy "Meato," who owns a chain of butcher shops. These stanzas capture his neurotic indecisiveness:

> I can't believe that I am fidgety
>
> Around Renee, and that the Meat King
> Her husband—that fat, that ignorant, that crass
> Wholesale butcher is what I really crave,
> That somewhere in me I am conjuring
> His slipping a long bratwurst up my ass!
> I am my mother's not my father's slave!
>
> I was attracted to Renee in school,
> Before the Meat King crawled into her bed.
> But then I wasn't rich enough, an heir,

Just a Momma's boy, a cheerleader, a fool.
But now, however, I am debonair,
A boy to flirt with, now that my father's dead. (41–42)

Ben is impatient with Larry's angst: "All day I hear my patients curse their fate, / How psychologically they recreate / Their parents' tyrannizing them with guilt / Until their penises refuse to tilt" (43). He advises Larry: "I don't speak glibly when I say rejoice, / Suffer your neuroses. But marry Joyce" (44). Joyce, however, has her own ideas. Addressing the psychiatrist later, she notes of his wife:

> Where's Mary? I hope she isn't ill. She
> Doesn't take much care of your . . . her body. Larry
> Is somewhere back there asking someone if
> He finally ought to take the plunge and marry.
> What do I want to do? Pour me a stiff
> Drink and I'll tell you. (49)

Joyce and Larry are not the only ones who seek out Ben's advice. Meato, the butcher, plans to send Renee to him: "I'm a man of wealth / Who'll pay what's necessary till this strife / Between us ends" (52). He observes her dancing with another man—"Look at what she does to me!" (53)—who encourages her to get even with her husband: "the way to slap her husband for the shrink—/ Sending he wants to do is piss / Him off right away by taking Larry for a ride / In Meato's big back-seated Rolls (Un!) Royce" (55).

At this point, the sequence veers away from the love storyline to discuss other characters, including a Yuppie headhunter (only metaphorically cannibalistic) "who's forced to work, / Eat, screw and read *The Wall Street Journal* in one / Room smaller than this living room" (62); the Guest of Honor, the rebel leader of Quistador; and Mark Stern, owner of a souvenir business. These serve mainly to articulate the feel of a cocktail party, but otherwise add little to the main story, which resumes with Ben—the psychiatrist—making a move of his own on a willing Joyce:

> Let's take my car and fill it up with gas
> And sit like teenagers together, ass to ass

And ride, who cares! tonight to Timbuktu.
I'll call my wife and tell her I love you,
And call my service, cancel everyone,
And you'll call Larry, call your mangy son,
And if somebody goes out of his mind . . .
We haven't much time left till we are dead.
Joyce, I'm tired of living in my head.
Get your bag, and leave your keys behind.
Come, help me dig my coat out of your bed.
It's nearly tomorrow now. It's time we fled. (72)

Similarly, Larry decides to put his engagement to Joyce out of its misery by leaving with Renee. He tells Ben, not yet knowing Ben has enticed Joyce:

What will happen to my life
If I give up my values, give up Joyce
And run away to Jersey with *his* wife?
Tell me I have a will. I have a choice,
That she is just my mother in disguise,
That I'm crossing my hands over my cock
Because her looking at me makes it rise,
Puts me in mortal terror of the clock.

She's given me ten minutes to decide,
The whimsical controlling little bitch.
She is the mob, taking me for a ride.
But I am going crazy with this itch!
Tell Joyce, my guest of honor—Honor!—I
Am fighting for my life and had to run,
That I am just an ordinary guy
Who wants the Prom Queen, wants to be twenty-one.
This dread is contagious. What about you?
You're my age, Ben. Stop me from what I'm going to do.
(73–74)

Renee's motives for leaving Meato are less mixed. Meato is lousy in bed:

> Didn't he say he's limp
> And thinks I'm a slut, impure
> For wanting sex? That oaf, that wimp,
> That king of everybody's meat
> But his—that's why he acts macho,
> Wrecking furniture when I cheat.
> Big man, grabbing a chair or table,
> Or going on t.v. as "Meato,"
> The hairy star of late-night cable. (75)

Larry summons Renee to go. Meanwhile, Joyce's son—who acknowledges he's gay—runs off to join the revolution in Quistador, even though the Guest of Honor collapses, drunk (83).

"The Psychiatrist's Epilogue" concludes the sequence in which Ben, the morning after, waxes philosophical on fate:

> No matter what religion we profess
> —Therapy, politics—we can only guess
> Our fates, and then they prove us wrong. The wheel
> Of Fortune must hand us a dirty deal.
> But in the meantime, let's watch the dust appear
> To dance in the sunlight, as I'm standing here,
> As last night, another life ago,
> We swore that we'd be young and simply go.
> But now that seems a gesture we have to make,
> Therapeutic, for our soul's or psyche's sake.
> You feel the same—to leave or not to leave,
> To rock and roll the moment that we grieve,
> Or else to find your son and me my wife,
> Return to an irrevocably altered life.
> What shall we do? says the Mentor to his Joyce.
> Be old or young again? What's your choice? (84–85)

This is, in one sense, an anti-climactic conclusion. No deep insight results. In part, however, that is the point of "The Psychiatrist at the Cocktail Party." The sequence is chiefly a satire of the shallow dimensions of contemporary culture, especially of mid-life adults; their evanescent relationships and casual politics. Love comes and goes; couples switch partners; no one fights for relationships or principles; life is adrift, unsettled. As Feirstein puts it in a critical afterword to *Ending the Twentieth Century:*

> The material I found myself drawn to over the past ten years had to do with a phenomenon many of us seemed to be experiencing, especially as we were moving toward middle age—that of deeply valuing our civilization and working for its continuity in an age that seemed to be in a mid-life crisis itself and frivolously divesting itself of its history, values and culture. (52)

What is love? What is worth fighting for? These characters are desperate to keep the energy of their youth and escape the misery of their middle-aged lives, even if they have to destroy everything to do so. But they have really lost, and gained, nothing; everything, and everyone, is interchangeable. As Ben asks Joyce: "Be old or young again? What's your choice?" That is the satiric point of "The Psychiatrist at the Cocktail Party." Though the poem is a witty portrait of a particular group of narcissistic, middle-aged urbanites, it is also more broadly applicable.

As Feirstein notes in the afterword to *Ending the Twentieth Century*, his vision of humanity shifted from comedic to tragic as he wrote the poems collected in his most recent volume: "as we moved through the eighties and into the nineties, the public losses we were imposing on ourselves began to feel like the repeated personal losses I'd been suffering" (52). The poems in *Ending the Twentieth Century* take deeply as their subject the end of the century; they consider the century's history in both personal and political terms. The book, like *City Life*, is divided into two sequences. "Manhattan Elegies and Other Goodbyes," the first part, moves primarily throughout the local landscapes of New York City. In "Creature of History," the focus is more historical, with the poems recording Feirstein's travels through Europe and his meditations on the bloody history of Europe in the twentieth century.

"Manhattan Elegy," which gives the first sequence its title, is chiefly a walk through memory. The poem is short enough to quote in full:

The past is like a library after dark
Where we sit on the steps trading stories
With characters we imagined ourselves to be.
Neighbors in clothing from our childhood stroll by,
Unmolested, nodding at us, benevolently.
One with your father's face tips his fedora.
You lower your eyes in shame. I look back.
Someone is sitting at a long table,
Reading in the moonlight. I must look startled.
He holds a forefinger to his lips
As if it is a candle for the dead.
You tap me on the shoulder and I turn back.
The street is dangerously empty
Except for the newsstand lit yellow,
Where your mother in a nightgown
Showing beneath her blue coat buys the *Times*,
A pack of *Kools* and, eyeing us, lights one.
You race to her, turn a corner. Goodbye.
I'm frightened, as if I am a foreigner
In a city under siege. Yet I know
It is still mid-century. Underground
Are only subways carrying boisterous
Party-goers or somber family men
Working the night shift or harmless bookies
Respectful of the No Smoking signs.
I walk to where the newsstand, shut,
Advertises brand names I'd forgotten.
I shove my hands into my pockets and whistle
A song we danced to when we were young.
I walk on for blocks, until I smell
Smoke from the burning borough of the Bronx. (7)

The poem, written in blank verse, draws an implicit contrast be-
tween the New York City of Feirstein's youth and the similar land-
scape today. Much has changed. Is it possible to imagine a safe,
polite subway in today's New York? Not likely. The poem's affection
for the past—the New York of the mid-twentieth-century—risks sen-
timentality, but stops short through its close scrutiny of the smallest

details of human life in 1950s New York. Indeed, the landscape is positively strange to Feirstein from his adult perspective: "I'm frightened, as if I am a foreigner." In a real sense, he is. Through its specifics of memory, the poem avoids the sentimental generalizations that are always the potential of elegies, especially poems that remember youth.

If "Manhattan Elegy" explores history and the past in personal terms, "Survivor," from the book's second half, shifts the focus to a larger perspective:

> Hid from Death, you collapse
> Into your father's armchair,
> As if in his arms, and ease
> Into the timid wisdom of middle age.
> You stare at your fruit trees where deer nibble,
> At the soft autumn sky, its cirrus clouds
> Drifting harmlessly as a child's thoughts,
> At your carefully tended perennial garden
> And abundant grape arbor and clipped lawn,
> Thinking how illusory you are,
> How shock weakens and repeated shock exhausts,
> And how, despite our knowledge and best intentions,
> Death repeatedly commits mayhem,
> Private and public, as in the newspaper on your lap
> Where Serbs slash breasts of women they've raped,
> Burn their children, castrate their husbands . . .
> You look away. Over the pine trees, your pine trees,
> A hawk lifts a screaming rabbit in its claws,
> Spiraling higher and higher into abstraction
> Like the numbers of dead in the newspaper
> Or the death-toll of your extended family:
> Mother, father, sister, uncle, aunts
> Who lived with you and had real names,
> Who sat laughing with you over pot roast
> And potatoes, red wine, and ginger ale
> In that mythic kitchen in your childhood home.
> Someone else's childhood. You look down at faces

Made of newsprint—shocked faces, grieving faces, accepting faces,
At cities like yours, sane in their architecture,
Efficient and health-conscious, except for the clouds
Of artillery smoke and gigantic Death,
Stepping between office towers, his machete
Real, sharp, relentless, indiscriminate. (49)

This poem is chiefly a meditation on the accidents of birth that
lead some people to lives of terror and death, and others to lives of
peace and prosperity. Feirstein alludes to some of the century's Eu-
ropean conflicts, including the bloodiness in Bosnia; he also alludes
to the Holocaust, which has touched his family, though Feirstein
himself is American-born. Death strikes, "real, sharp, relentless, in-
discriminate," yet it has missed Feirstein, who watches deer nibble
the leaves of fruit trees near his lawn, a place as far from the blood
of history as one could imagine. The poem's clarity and brisk for-
malism make its points especially effectively.

Both "Manhattan Elegy" and "Survivor," while fine poems in
their own rights, attain additional resonance through their place-
ment in sequences. They both establish and elaborate dimensions of
the sequence's themes. The poems are undoubtedly more somber
—"serious" is not the appropriate word—than the satire of "The
Psychiatrist at the Cocktail Party," reflecting the progressive darken-
ing of Feirstein's vision over the past decade. To Feirstein's credit, he
has worked hard to find the appropriate structure to explore his vi-
sion in depth. In fact, his work is more compelling, read in length,
rather than in small doses. In the book's afterword, he explains the
appeal of the sequence mode: "The poetic sequence seemed more
flexible and expansive. It allows the poet to expand out from the self,
and enables him or her to use a variety of genres—particularly the
meditative, lyric and shorter narrative—and to combine them into a
drama in which a protagonist journeys through both inner and
outer worlds simultaneously" (52).

Ultimately, Feirstein's work is distinctive for the range of its
drama and the depth of its vision. He is less a narrative than a dra-
matic poet, in the sense that story is less important to his poetry

than the portrayal of character and the exploration of ideas. His use of the sequence gives his work its distinctive depth, and the brisk formalism of his poems allows him to develop character and idea with crisp directness.

The Satirist's Eye: R.S. Gwynn

If a satirist is a wounded idealist, one who painfully recognizes the contrast between the world as it is and the world as it should be, then R.S. Gwynn (born 1948) is a satirist's satirist. In several books— *Bearing and Distance* (1977), *The Narcissiad* (1981), *The Drive-In* (1986), *Body Bags* (1990), *The Area Code of God* (1993), and *No Word of Farewell* (1996)—Gwynn looks savagely at the world's follies, mocking them with a sharpness that few contemporary poets display. Yet he is also capable of compassion and humor when he deals with moments when life comes close to what it should be. And Gwynn explores this wide range of subjects and tones in an even wider range of styles: he freely mixes intellectual urbanity with low, even coarse, humor and language; and his work is crisply formal, making use of a variety of metrical and rhyme schemes. As Lisa Russ Spaar notes of Gwynn: "This is a poetry of startling juxtapositions, of slaps in the face, nudges in the ribs, of audacity and even courage" (2). Gwynn's particular combination of strengths makes him almost unique among his generation, and part of a small group of poets of the past three decades.

A short direct example of Gwynn's technique is "Scenes from the Playroom," from his most prominent collection, *The Drive-In*:

> Now Lucy with her family of dolls
> Disfigures Mother with an emery board,
> While Charles, with match and rubbing alcohol,
> Readies the struggling cat, for Chuck is bored.
> The young ones pour more ink into the water
> Through which the latest goldfish gamely swims,
> Laughing, pointing at naked, neutered Father.
> The toy chest is a Buchenwald of limbs.

Mother is so lovely; Father, so late.
The cook is off, yet dinner must go on.
With onions as her only cause for tears
She hacks the red meat from the slippery bone,
Setting the table, while the children wait,
Her grinning babies, clean behind the ears. (26)

This sonnet skewers the stereotypical middle-class family merci-
lessly. The children are spoiled, the toy chest a killing field. The fa-
ther is late, either at work or adultery, so the mother—who has sent
the family cook home—must prepare dinner alone. She has no real
cause for tears except from the onions she slices—or so we think. Her
actions reveal otherwise. She does not just cut the meat, she hacks at
it; this is the action of tightly controlled rage. Although she lives in an
affluent household and her children are clean behind the ears—what
more can a mother want?—she is clearly unhappy. Through his sub-
tle use of detail, Gwynn develops a compassionate undercurrent to
the mock-horrific scene.

A more complex example of Gwynn's technique is "Among
Philistines," the opening poem of *The Drive-In*. The poem takes as
its subject Samson and Delilah, but places them in the media culture
of late-twentieth-century America. (The lines I quote are from the
poem's most recent version in Gwynn's short selected poems, *No
Word of Farewell*.) Because he killed multitudes with the jawbone of
an ass, Samson is now a celebrity of talk shows and tabloids, while
Delilah displays her wares for soft-core films:

After a word for douche, Delilah made
A live appearance and was interviewed.
Complaining what a pittance she was paid,
She plugged the film she starred in in the nude.

Unbearable, he thought, and flipped the switch,
Lay sleepless on the bed in the bright room
Where every thought brought back the pretty bitch
And all the Orient of her perfume,

Her perfect breasts, her lips and slender waist,
Matchless among the centerfolds of Zion,

> Which summoned to his tongue the mingled taste
> Of honey oozing from the rotted lion. (15)

Samson still considers himself a serious, even studious man, not a sex object, and wants no part of the business he has entered:

> Beefcake aside, he was a man of thought
> Who heretofore had kept to the strict law;
> For all the cheap celebrity it brought
> He honestly deplored that ass's jaw,
>
> The glossy covers of their magazines
> With taut chains popping on his greasy chest,
> The ads for razor blades with the staged scenes
> And captions: *Hebrew Hunk Says We Shave Best!* (16)

Samson can only observe Delilah with disgust:

> And this last image, *this,* mile upon mile:
> Delilah, naked, sucking on a pair
> Of golden shears, winking her lewdest smile
> Amid a monumental pile of hair
>
> And blaring type: *Meet the Babe Who Skinned the Yid!*
> *Starring in JUST A LITTLE OFF MY HEAD.*
> He noted how his locks demurely hid
> Those monstrous tits. And how her lips were red. (16)

As in the Biblical story, Samson is led to his death. But among these Philistines, death is "a blessing in disguise. / 'Good riddance,' he said, whispering to the pain / As searing, the twin picks hissed in his eyes" (17).

Written in rhymed, iambic pentameter quatrains, "Among Philistines" is a rich satire of contemporary culture. The title, of course, is drawn directly from the Biblical story of Samson and Delilah, but also has a contemporary edge: the Philistines of this poem are the media vultures and their addle-minded audience. And living in such culture is especially painful for Samson. For him, death would be a release. The poem's blend of high and low culture, of intellectual irony and dirty joke, are especially effective.

While satire is Gwynn's usual style, he is capable of writing lyrics of great delicacy. The title poem of *The Drive-In* is a particularly good example. Written in iambic tetrameter rhymed couplets, the poem begins with the speaker's eager anticipation of the drive-in movie with his family:

> Under the neon sign he stands,
> My father, tickets in his hands.
> Now it is my turn; all the while
> Knee-deep in stubs he tries to smile,
> Crying, "You'll love it. Slapstick. Fights.
> One dollar, please. Please dim your lights."
> I pay and enter. Mother waits
> In a black truck with dangle plates
> And snag-toothed grillwork idling there
> On the front row. She combs her hair
> And calls for me to take my place. (39)

The poem rehearses the terror and thrill of the movies: "And now the feature has begun: / *Union Pacific* is its name. / I know it, know it frame by frame" (39).

And the poem has this rich conclusion, when the speaker's perspective shifts from childhood to adulthood:

> I fall asleep. The night is cold.
> And waking to the seat's chill touch
> I hear the last car's slipping clutch,
> As on the glass a veil of frost
> Obscures this childhood I have lost.
> The show is over. Time descends.
> And no one tells me how it ends. (40)

In these last couplets, the poem depicts not only the end of a childhood evening, but the end of a childhood. "No one tells me how it ends"—childhood simply gives way gradually to adulthood as time slowly passes. The poem's smooth formality and understatement turn a common, potentially mawkish subject to one of considerable power.

At times, Gwynn tempers his satirical poems with the delicacy of "The Drive-In." A significant example is "Approaching a Significant Birthday, He Peruses the *Norton Anthology of Poetry*," from *Body Bags*. The poem is worth quoting in full, here in its *No Word of Farewell* version:

> All human things are subject to decay.
> Beauty is momentary in the mind.
> The curfew tolls the knell of parting day.
> If Winter comes, can Spring be far behind?
>
> Forlorn! the very word is like a bell
> And somewhat of a sad perplexity.
> Here, take my picture, though I bid farewell,
> In a dark time the eye begins to see
>
> The woods decay, the woods decay and fall—
> Bare ruined choirs where late the sweet birds sang.
> What but design of darkness to appall?
> An aged man is but a paltry thing.
>
> If I should die, think only this of me:
> Crass casualty obstructs the sun and rain
> When I have fears that I may cease to be,
> To cease upon the midnight with no pain
>
> And hear the spectral singing of the moon
> And strictly meditate the thankless muse.
> The world is too much with us, late and soon.
> It gathers to a greatness, like the ooze.
>
> Do not go gentle into that good night.
> Fame is no plant that grows on mortal soil.
> Again he raised the jug up to the light:
> Old age hath yet his honor and his toil.
>
> Downward to darkness on extended wings,
> Break, break, break, on thy cold gray stones, O sea,
> And tell sad stories of the death of kings.
> I do not think that they will sing to me. (36–37)

This poem demonstrates Gwynn's intellectual erudition, formal skill, and sense of humor. The poem, as any reader of the *Norton Anthology* will see, is composed of lines lifted from other canonical poems, and forged into a context at once old and new—the meditation of an aged man. While in one sense this is unoriginal—Gwynn does not so much write the poem as arrange it—Gwynn fashions these various fragments, drawn from numerous poets (including Eliot, Keats, Shakespeare, Stevens, Thomas, Wordsworth, and others) over several centuries, into a seamless whole, in which the poem gently mocks the speaker's middle-aged fears in heroic quatrains. This is no mean feat.

Gwynn is a sharp satirist, but as his "anthology" poem (itself anthologized) and "The Drive-In" demonstrate, he does not lack compassion or humor. Instead, he uses a broad range of forms to cast a watchful, often skeptical eye on contemporary culture. He is not a prolific poet, but he is a consistently fine one. The particular features of his work—its blend of high and low reference, its formal resources, and the richness of its satire—are unlike any other Expansive poet, and unlike most poets of the past several decades. (In the generation preceding his, the poets most resembling Gwynn are X.J. Kennedy and W.D. Snodgrass, both mavericks. Though Snodgrass is correctly associated with the Confessional poets—he basically invented the mode—his *Selected Poems* are vastly wider ranging than Confessionalism.) Gwynn demonstrates that satire remains a viable, valuable mode of poetry, and his own age provides no shortage of subjects for his scrutiny.

The Hard Ironies of History: Charles Martin

In "Reading the New Formalists," Robert McPhillips says of Charles Martin (born 1942):

> Charles Martin . . . impresses one with his intelligence, the range of his interests, the technical mastery of his verse. . . . But . . . Martin's poetry labors more heavily under the burden of its erudition. In

Martin's case, this learning ultimately proves a strength, but it also renders his verse less immediately likable and accessible. (314)

Martin is a poet of unabashed erudition and formality, and yet his poetry is not the same as the 1950s formalists. His intelligence is not displayed in the obscurity of his allusions or the audacity of his formal ornamentation, but instead in the unusual range of his subjects, the effortlessness of his formal work, and the seriousness, even gravity, of his poems. One characteristic example of Martin's technique is "Terminal Colloquy," from his first book, *Room for Error* (1978):

O where will you go when the blinding flash
Scatters the seed of a million suns?
And what will you do in the rain of ash?

I'll draw the blinds and pull down the sash,
And hide from the light of so many noons.
But how will it be when the blinding flash

Disturbs your body's close-knit mesh,
Bringing light to your lovely bones?
What will you wear in the rain of ash?

I will go bare without my flesh,
My vertebrae will click like stones.
Ah. But where will you dance when the blinding flash

Settles the city in a holy hush?
I will dance alone among the ruins.
Ah. And what will you say to the rain of ash?

I will be charming. My subtle speech
Will weave close turns and counter turns—
No. What will you say to the rain of ash?
Nothing, after the blinding flash. (14)

A better title for this poem might be "Apocalyptic Villanelle." It offers an excellent example of Martin's technique. The poem uses the repeating lines of the villanelle to suggest at once the surreal beauty of a nuclear blast and its obscene aftermath. Martin's juxtaposition of these extreme contrasts in the formal grace of a villanelle is jolting, rather than witty, irony; it suggests both his formal resources and his intellectual interests, which are frequently historical and political. This poem, published when the Cold War and fears of nuclear apocalypse were the order of the day, is especially effective.

Another compelling poem in *Room for Error* is a sequence, "Four for Theodore Roethke." The sequence is an homage to Roethke's life and poetry, drawing on images, themes, phrases and even the forms of Roethke's work. Part I, "The Circle," addresses Roethke's fundamental stance toward poetry: "He loved the edges, where the changes are." Whether writing of love, nature, or his difficult relationship with his father, Roethke was a poet of exquisite sensitivity to the world, which he recorded with great delicacy in his lines:

> Standing at the center of his field
> He brought us news of all insensible things,
> The near, deep lives of another world:
> Nudged by beginnings, echoes drew him out;
> Inevitable endings cut him short. (16)

Part II, "The Garden," recalls Roethke's father, a greenhouse keeper whose work greatly influenced Roethke's later poetry. While Roethke famously memorialized his father's roughness in "My Papa's Waltz," the wild, natural images that he recalled from his father's greenhouse became a central image of his poetry:

> But in the canceled greenhouse of his memory
> Where it was summer throughout the year,
> The vast, unmeasured outside let him be,
> And even death backed down, speechless before
> The iron mandate of his father's will. (17)

Martin notes that beyond the greenhouse was "A world of endless, varied sequence; he / Bent to it, like a lover, secretly" (17).

Part III, "The Dance," extends Roethke's love of the physical world into other forms of love—human love, and love of poetry. A female figure in this section, perhaps the muse or Roethke's own life, dances with him; this section recalls Roethke's wonderful love poems from the 1950s, written with a Yeatsian formality that the entire sequence echoes: "He knew her body's risk, his body's task: / Wild shape took shape behind a formal mask" (18). Part IV, "The Burden," alludes more directly to the end of Roethke's life, when he discovered happiness in marriage and wrote his best poems—the Yeatsian love poems of *Words for the Wind* and the Whitmanian sequences of *The Far Field*. This section is worth quoting in whole:

> The burden flowering at heavy cost:
> He knew the cost, knew how the burgeoning
> Bough shudders in the wind, already lost—
> And the heavy price paid when the opening
> Buds become the blossoms on a tree;
> These blossoms ripen and they break their bough.
>
> No longer pacing out his middle age,
> He tumbled quickly to an ecstasy,
> He loosened into love, that purest rage,
> Impossible to risk or justify;
> Circumference was never more than here
> And now, no end was on it, anywhere—
>
> There was no edge, there was no edge at all!
> He knew the virtue of some secret name,
> It was impossible for him to fall:
> Bobbing like a blossom on a stem
> He was indifferent to all but joy,
> And with his words he gave himself away:
>
> Inside the cherry is the lightest stone,
> But nonetheless the cherry's branches cry
> Out at its weight: they cannot bear for long
> The burden of their joy. No more could he.
> That heavy body bore a glistening word.
> Now fold his hands away, misunderstood. (19)

A gorgeous, elegiac conclusion, "The Burden" sums up a central theme in Roethke's poetry, expressed in these lines: "I bear, but not alone,/The burden of this joy." True peace in the world is tremendously difficult to achieve; love of the world and other human beings, and art, can help one manage the burden of such joy.

McPhillips identifies *Room for Error* as perhaps the earliest mature example of New Formalist poetry, but notes that the book received little attention (314). (Another candidate might be Frederick Feirstein's *Survivors,* which appeared in 1975.) *Steal the Bacon* (1987), published nine years later, features many of the same strengths as Martin's first book, but is also impressive for some ambitious new experiments with narrative and the dramatic monologue—particularly the book's longest poem, "Passages from Friday."

"Passages from Friday" retells the story of Robinson Crusoe from the perspective of his black servant, Friday. The poem is told in Friday's words; Martin shapes the eighteenth-century voice, complete with Friday's occasional clumsiness with language, into smooth, rhymed iambic quatrains. This requires extreme formal dexterity, which Martin displays from the outset in introducing Friday:

> With my owne thoro' un-Worthyness
> all ways befor my Face I turn to
> this burthensom Task which neertheless
> being decided, *Viz.* That I must learn to
>
> write as my *Master* did & so set down
> tho' withow any Hope of Recovery
> from this inchanted Island to my owne
> Nation whence taken in Captivity
>
> som Yeers a go: (24)

The difference between Crusoe and Friday becomes evident immediately. Though Crusoe is dependent on Friday for his survival, he regards him as a servant, and treats him cruelly:

> How each Day was spent
> from 1st Light, when I go off to gather
> Fewel for the Fire lay'd owt Side his Tent
>
> then fetch his Cloathes for him & lay them owt:
> *Then leve him be now:* run off to prepare
> his Goats-Flesh Stewe; this done, I hear him showt:
> *Bring him his Jugg;* I fetch it in & pour
>
> him a great Supp to drink, whilst he dresses
> & then attend him till his Stewe is eaten

> & then if all has not been as he pleases
> as like as not poor *Friday* will get beaten; (26-27)

Still, Friday proves a faithful partner, and together the two design a craft that Crusoe hopes will liberate them from the island. The canoe, though, is detroyed in their attempt. Crusoe, despondent, enters into a mental decline, and later is fatally injured in a fall:

> he was incapable of Movement or Speech;
> I did What little I cou'd do for him
> there & then carry'd him down to the Beach,
> & then, the next day, by easy Stages Home.
>
> Despite my Care for him, he did not regayn
> any of thos Powers lost in his Fall;
> since Death was certain, I told him of my Plan;
> viz., that incertain of *Christian* Buriall,
>
> not having yet been taught by him in this,
> but at the same Time, being a *Heathen* no more,
> I had som Notions of the Sacrifice
> & Ceremony proper to ensure
>
> his Souls release. (42–43)

"Passages from Friday" is a remarkable achievement for several reasons. First, it re-animates a well-known story—that of Crusoe—from a different perspective. Crusoe, far from the resourceful, heroic survivor of legend, emerges here as arrogant and manipulative, a man of intelligence and skill but also cruelty—a man who is utterly dependent on Friday, but because of his time and status (white sailor with black servant) is unable to treat Friday as an equal, although he does at times treat him with affection. Friday deserves Crusoe's affection, because he is intelligent, resourceful and patient with Crusoe's outbursts. Yet Friday is a complex character; he notes the numerous instances of Crusoe beating him for no better reason than irritation. Friday is proud as well as patient, and he struggles to maintain his dignity in an unequal partnership that manipulates his compassion a great deal. Implicitly, the poem has a great deal to say about the issue of race through its portrayal of Friday's complex humanity—a humanity that Crusoe largely denies.

"Passages from Friday" is a striking formal achievement as well as a compelling dramatic monologue and exploration of historical and racial issues. Martin's decision to have Friday speak in an eighteenth-century voice is appropriate, but poses obvious risks—either of the condescension that can accompany the use of dialect, or not being faithful to the conventions of the dialect, or not being able to fit the dialect into formal measures. Remarkably, Martin avoids all these pitfalls. In his hands, Friday's voice is consistent and appropriate and wholly in harmony with the metrical and rhyme schemes. "Passages from Friday" is one of the central poems of Martin's achievement.

One of the other significant poems of *Steal the Bacon* is the stunning "Easter Sunday, 1985," a sonnet:

> *To take steps toward the reappearance alive of the disap-*
> *peared is a subversive act, and measures will be adopted to deal*
> *with it.*
> > —General Oscar Mejia Victores, President of Guatemala

In the Palace of the President this morning,
The General is gripped by the suspicion
That those who were disappeared will be returning
In a subversive act of resurrection.

Why do you worry? The disappeared can never
Be brought back from wherever they were taken;
The age of miracles is gone forever;
These are not sleeping, nor will they awaken.

And if some tell you Christ once reappeared
Alive, one Easter morning, that he was seen—
Give them the lie, for who today can find him?

He is perhaps with those who were disappeared,
Broken and killed, flung into some ravine
With his arms safely wired up behind him. (53)

In "Toward a Liberal Poetics," Paul Lake calls this one of Martin's finest poems, praising its "refreshing boldness and subtlety on the larger issues of our time" (121). What is most striking about this poem is that it can support at least two related, but different, political readings. Read simply as a straightforward expression of despair

—the image of the crucified Jesus among "the disappeared"—the poem has an obvious power. Yet when read with an awareness of the ironies prevalent in Martin's work, almost the opposite reading becomes possible. The poem states that resurrection is impossible; and yet this statement is made literally on Easter Sunday. Can resurrection really be impossible on Easter, the day of Christ's resurrection? Against all hope, might there actually be something for the military junta to fear? Why is the general/president forbidding the reappearance of the disappeared, anyway? The poem raises but does not answer such questions; nor does it resolve which reading is the more valid one. Perhaps (and this would be characteristic of Martin) both readings are possible. The former is dark, the latter even darker, about a topic of fundamental importance: the political murder of human beings.

Martin's most recent book, *What the Darkness Proposes* (1996), is something of a disappointment, especially compared to *Steal the Bacon*. The book's centerpiece is a long poem, "A Walk in the Hills Above the Artists' House"—an extended meditation on, of all things, the life and work of art as viewed from an artists' colony, a well-funded, bucolic retreat where artists—writers, painters, sculptors, composers—may work in leisure and isolation.

Here is a selection from the poem's beginning:

1/

Late afternoon: in studios
Where work is done or unbegun,
Disoriented poets close
The books on rough draft or revision,
Outside, as a declining sun
Takes aim at the Pacific Ocean,
A little clearing slowly fills
With those who'd like to walk the hills

2/

Above the temporary quarters
(Emptying out for the hike)
Where composers, artists, writers
Have settled in to make their mark,

Each different but all alike
In having gotten time to work
As much or as little as we please,
And walk sometime among the trees—

    3/
Perhaps the same trees I flew over
After I managed to exchange
My sweaty feedbag for the clover
Of a few weeks' idleness;
Significant others find it strange,
But work that any artist does
Paradoxically depends
On leisure to achieve its ends. (23–24)

Though these stanzas are elegantly written, one can scarcely imagine a more self-indulgent topic for a poet: a 30-page meditation on the artist's leisured life, subsidized by private foundations or the state. When one considers the moral gravity and resonance of Martin's best poetry, his interest in this topic—treated with a seriousness that borders on self-parody—becomes even more mystifying. And the rest of the book does not compensate for this poem; the rest of *What the Darkness Proposes* contains an assortment of urbane, witty poems that, while skillful, do not redeem the failure of the artist colony poem.

Perhaps the best poem in the book is "Victoria's Secret":

Victorian mothers instructed their daughters, ahem,
That whenever their husbands were getting it off on them,
The only thing for it was just to lie perfectly flat
And try to imagine themselves out buying a new hat;
So, night after night, expeditions grimly set off,
Each leaving a corpse in its wake to service the toff
With the whiskers and whiskey, the lecherous ogre bent
Over her, thrashing and thrusting until he was spent.
Or so we imagine, persuaded that our ancestors
Couldn't have been as brightly unbuttoned as we are,
As our descendants will shun the kinds of repression
They think we were prone to, if thinking comes back into fashion.
And here is *Victoria's Secret*, which fondly supposes

That the young women depicted in various poses
Of complaisant negligence somehow or other reveal
More than we see of them: we're intended to feel
That this simply isn't a matter of sheer lingerie,
But rather the baring of something long hidden away
Being an outmoded conception of rectitude:
Liberation appears to us, not entirely nude,
In the form of a fullbreasted nymph, implausibly slim,
Airbrushed at each conjunction of torso and limb,
Who looks up from the page with large and curious eyes
That never close: and in their depths lie frozen
The wordless dreams shared by all merchandise,
Even the hats that wait in the dark to be chosen. (7)

This poem, drawing an unexpected parallel between the historic repressiveness of Victorian England and its contemporary, commercialized re-creation in the Victoria's Secret lingerie store, is a good example of his piercing irony—one of the few such examples in the book.

The focus of so much of *What the Darkness Proposes* on the writing act, the power of literature, and other dimensions of the *ars poetica*, is puzzling. Martin's intent seems to be to meditate on the nature of art, its relationship to audience, and the conditions of art's production. Yet Martin's imagination seems ill-suited to such meditation. One wonders if these poems emerged from a frustrated dry spell (one poem is titled "Reflections After a Dry Spell"). If so, perhaps they are simply an interlude to stronger work. Poems such as "Victoria's Secret" remind a reader just how good Martin's best work is. Martin remains a poet of wide intellectual and formal resources—of all the Expansive poets, his work probably poses the most challenges for a reader. Ultimately, Martin's formal grace and his understanding of history's hard ironies make his poetry among the most substantial achievements of the Expansive school and, more importantly, of his generation.

7

Expansive Influence

The Exhaustion of University Poetry

In its two decades of existence, the Expansive poetry movement has achieved a great deal, producing a maturing body of poetry that has renewed and enhanced traditions in form and narrative while extending the range of possibilities of style and subject in contemporary poetry. Many of the poets associated with the movement have also written an accessible body of criticism that challenges the complex body of ideas associated with Postmodernism and invigorates neglected questions of prosody and narrative technique in verse. Finally, the Expansive poets have played a leading role in arguing for poetry's emergence from an academic subculture to a position of greater importance in American life.

Indeed, by 1991, the squabble over the relationship between poetry and the university was already becoming old news. The preceding few years had seen many salvos: Diane Wakoski's 1986 attack on the emerging formalist movement; the 1988 special issue of *Crosscurrents* edited by Dick Allen; Joseph Epstein's vitriolic 1988 essay in *Commentary,* "Who Killed Poetry?"; the chorus of boos against Epstein from poet-professors in a 1989 *AWP Chronicle;* the

1989 publication of *Expansive Poetry*, the movement's testy manifesto that argues in part to expand poetry's audience beyond the university (even though some Expansive poets are professors); the 1990 publication of Expansive poet-professor Timothy Steele's *Missing Measures*, which regards the free verse legacy of Modernism (the underpinning of the "university poetry" Expansive poets criticize) as an experiment gone dreadfully wrong; the 1990 publication of Robert McDowell's anthology, *Poetry After Modernism*, which includes essays on poetry, audience, and the university by McDowell, Bruce Bawer and others; the 1991 appearance of Gioia's essay "Can Poetry Matter?" in *The Atlantic*, which asserted that poetry, under the university's patronage, has lost its cultural relevance; another chorus of boos from poet-professors (non-Expansive) in *The Atlantic*—and, interestingly, a chorus of cheers from general readers.

The particular shape of this debate—among Expansive poets and the academic creative writing establishment—is a good measure of Expansive poetry's influence. (As I note in Chapter II, the Expansive poets have had less influence among literary theorists and critics, who have little to do with academic creative writers.) For the most part, the debate has been defined and conducted on Expansive poetry's terms. The criticism of Expansive poetry by university creative writing faculty has frequently lacked rigor. This is, in part, because MFA programs, governed by a neo-Romantic ideology that focuses on the development of a writer's craft (or "individual voice") over a systematic historical and theoretical grounding in literature, do not typically equip their graduates with extensive experience in critical discourse.

In this debate, the most significant response to the Expansive poets' critique of poetry and the university has been Jonathan Holden's *The Fate of American Poetry* (1991). It is significant, first, simply because of its author. Holden, University Distinguished Professor at Kansas State University, is as establishment a poet-professor as it is possible to be; he has published seven books of poetry, all with university presses, and has won most of the major university poetry awards in his career (the Devins, Associated Writing Programs and Juniper prizes). Moreover, Holden is one of the few major academic poets who is also a significant critic; he has published critical studies of William Stafford and Richard Hugo, and two essay collections on poetry that are important contributions to upholding the contemporary free-verse aesthetic. If any free-verse poet-professor has a substantial critical argument to make, it is Holden.

The Fate of American Poetry is the most substantial argument the non-Expansive side has offered. But what the book ultimately shows is just how comprehensive the Expansive critique of the university writing establishment has been. Holden's book attempts to defend the status quo by accepting the terms set forth by the Expansive poets and others; it attempts to answer those attacking the university's patronage of poetry on their own ground. In doing so, it advances a provocative, but finally unconvincing, thesis: after conceding that poetry has been marginalized in the twentieth century and admitting that there is a tremendous amount of mediocre verse written today, he veers radically away from critics such as Steele and Gioia by arguing that the university is the key to restoring poetry's relevance, rather than the cause of its irrelevance.

In Holden's view, the post-World War II explosion in university enrollments has resulted in the democratization of high culture, making it accessible to more people than ever before. Furthermore, he says, as high literacy continues to decline in America, the university as an institution has taken over patronage of all types of intellectual reading, not just poetry. He asks: "Isn't it self-evident that the benefits of having universities to provide a reasonably stable patronage, not just for poets but for that dwindling percentage of our population devoted to reading, greatly outweigh the disadvantages?" (13).

Holden blames Modernism and its emphasis on formal innovation, its equation of form with content, for driving readers away from poetry. He argues that while much of Modernism—Eliot's doctrine of impersonality and the dauntingly intellectual nature of much Modernist poetry—has passed into literary history, the notion that linguistic genius supersedes all else "persists as a kind of [M]odernist hangover, one epitomized infamously in MacLeish's dictum, 'a poem must not mean/but be'" (51–52).

Typically, lyric poetry working with this last tenet of Modernism

—derived from Williams as well as Eliot, whose phrase "art-emo-tion" Holden cites—avoids any kind of direct statement, preferring instead to present clear images, implicit emotion, and quietly ele-gant, free-verse language in a mode that David Dooley calls the "contemporary workshop aesthetic" (260). While such poetry may seem natural and "organic," Holden argues that its effect "is mainly literary, an Eliotian 'art-emotion'—an effect of such artificiality and refinement that in order to receive it at all one would have to have undergone extensive pedagogical indoctrination" (58).

Holden believes that the "democratization" of poetry—both in its production and its content—in the 1960s and 1970s has been cru-cial in overturning Modernist elitism, making poetry more accessi-ble, and increasing its audience. He traces these developments through the founding of the National Endowment for the Arts, the burgeoning expansion of university creative writing programs, and the development of Confessional and Deep Image poetry, in which content—personal problems and the archetypal subconscious—is theoretically open to everyone. He also cites, approvingly, a partial backlash against these two poetic modes in the late 1970s.

Holden approves of the expansion of literary modes available to poets, because he believes that is the key to regaining a widespread interest in poetry. He seeks to recapture subject matter that the Modernists had conceded to prose. In Holden's words, verse "can accommodate with surprising fluency the types of subject matter we find in novels, sermons, and essays. In fact, verse, through its structural conventions and prosodic capabilities, can present this subject matter differently than the other competing genres can, but with its own kind of charm" (14–15).

Holden believes that the possibilities for formal innovation on the scale of the Modernists are nil. He dismisses Expansive poetry, erroneously, as a throwback to 1950s formalism, and argues that the key to poetic innovation in the near future—and to further expand-ing poetry's reading audience—lies in new subject matter: didactic, discursive and narrative poetry, which revive "the entire range of poetic conventions that had been curbed by the imagistic, show-don't-tell pieties of the [M]odernist tradition" (107). The bulk of the book is devoted to examining representative contemporary poems and suggesting how other poets might emulate them. Attacking Epstein's essay "Who Killed Poetry?" in particular, Holden complains that Epstein succumbs "to what is probably the most insidious temptation for a critic—the temptation to scan the forest, make grand generalizations about it, while losing sight of the trees" (14). Holden's critiques of contemporary poems work hard to avoid this shortcoming, but he is far less successful when it comes to explaining how the university is the key to expanding poetry's readership. In order to do so, Holden must show how the Expansive poets' arguments are wrong, how they miss the point. This he fails to do. Instead, he drops the issue, never suggesting specific ways universities *as institutions* can attract a wider audience for poetry. After putting forth his argument that the democratization of higher education has widened the university audience for poetry, Holden explicitly assumes that there is no longer an audience for poetry *outside* the university: "The issue facing poets was not how to get poetry out of the classroom. The university classroom was an appropriate place for it, the main place where books—not just poetry—were seriously read" (49).

As a response to the Expansive poets' critique, this is incredibly myopic, smug, or both. Does Holden believe there is no audience for poetry, or for *any* kind of serious art or reading, outside the university? Should he not at least acknowledge that, for instance, while the university plays a leading role in serious literacy, poets can share their work in public libraries, in art galleries, in bookstores, in bars, in homeless shelters? These venues attract people other than students or professors. It does not undermine his central point about the good the university has done for poetry in the past 30 years—and that good has been abundant—to concede that there is no need for the university to maintain a stranglehold on poetry. If American poetry under the university's patronage is "more vigorous than at any time in American history," as Holden insists (49), then why write a book suggesting ways to renovate it—particularly with ideas that have been put forth by a number of other poets as well? The answer, though never explicitly stated in *The Fate of American Poetry*, is implied throughout the book: the dominant aesthetic of university poetry in the past 20 years, of which Holden is a major practitioner, is exhausted.

Holden has a great allegiance to his own tradition of poetry, which in an earlier book, *Style and Authenticity in Postmodern Poetry*, he called a "'vernacular poetry of personal ethos,' a low mimetic mode of poetry" (5). Since its inception in the early 1970s, this "vernacular" poetry has been influential. In *The Fate of American Poetry*, Holden places this tradition in the middle of the poetic political spectrum, "its main and central strand . . . continuing the liberal, humanistic and egalitarian cultural projects of the 1960s and 70s" (30); he clearly believes this is the most important kind of contemporary poetry. This is the type of poetry Holden has spent his career writing, and championing as a critic. In *Style and Authenticity in Postmodern Poetry*, he defines it in detail:

> These poems are not exclusively about their own language or their own formal properties. They are not narrowly personal or confessional; neither are they impersonal. They evoke some sense of an authorial presence behind their words. More than that: this presence, this personality is better than what we are accustomed to in daily life. We sense a substantial, personal ethos behind the language, that the rhetoric is in the service of serious and worthwhile intentions. This authorial presence is one we trust. It is sincere. (5–6)

What Holden describes here is, in fact, a major strand of David Dooley's "contemporary workshop aesthetic," the part Dooley classifies as the "domesticated confessional" (260). The imagistic lyrics that Holden so disdains make up part of that aesthetic, but so does this "vernacular poetry of personal ethos" that Holden champions. It is not *narrowly* personal or confessional, but nonetheless features some version of the author grappling with the difficulties of day-to-day living; it typically features a modesty of language and subject matter, depending precisely on the "sincerity" of the authorial voice to attract readers. Rather than aiming at grand pronouncements or grand subjects, note Dave Smith and David Bottoms in their *Morrow Anthology of Younger American Poets*, "the younger poet tends to be himself, an invented version of himself. . . . His knowledge, while eclectic, seems focused on the psychological and mythological resonance in the local surface, event, or subject" (19).

Here is an example of Holden's own work in this mode. "The Swimming Pool" was first published in his second book, *Leverage* (1982), and later reprinted in Smith and Bottoms's anthology (which Gioia has called "not so much a selective literary collection as a comprehensive directory of creative-writing teachers" [*Can Poetry Matter?* (8)]):

> Long after he'd wearied of the work
> I recall my father sloshing in hip boots,
> ignoring the mosquitoes on his back
> to lay by hand, around the stone
> swimming pool he'd built, this tile
> drain to divert the brook when it
> turned brown in thunderstorms, how
> he grunted as he pried up each sucking
> shovelful of muck, his face
> a shiny little mask of wrinkled sweat,
> hating every minute of it.
> And I remember how, later, in July,
> when the wet heat would make you
> claustrophobic and despair
> he'd step up to that pool—
> shy almost—gingerly dip in a toe,
> exclaim wryly, then begin the ritual,
> first rinse the arms,
> then wash the chest,
> his legs meanwhile feeling their way
> on tiptoe as he waded forward, becoming
> shorter and shorter, the cold lip
> of the water crawling up his stomach
> until, ready to receive the cold,
> he'd lie back on his back and sigh,

> then close his eyes as though
> that pool could never give him back
> enough or fast enough or long enough
> all that he'd put into it. (317)

This poem bears out every generalization that Smith and Bottoms make. Holden here recollects his childhood, and more specifically his father. His father literally delves below the "local surface" of the pool he built, making himself clean after a day of hard summer work. It is a common suburban activity, but Holden locates the larger resonance of the scene. The pool, and implicitly, everything else in that home, could never "give him back / enough." The poem mixes nostalgia with regret; in its way, it asks what to make of a diminished thing. "The Swimming Pool" is a good example of Holden's "vernacular" poetry.

So what is wrong with this tradition? By itself, nothing. It has produced a body of serious work in the past two decades by poets as diverse as Richard Hugo, William Stafford, Sharon Olds, Carolyn Forché, and Stephen Dunn, as well as Holden himself. But any style of poetry will have its time of energy and invention, then slowly harden into mannerisms. The "vernacular" mode is no different. Even Holden, who still defends this tradition in his criticism, rejects it in his more recent poetry. *Against Paradise* (1990), *American Gothic* (1992), and *The Sublime* (1996) move past the sincere, personal lyric of his earlier work toward the didactic, discursive, and narrative styles he now advocates, without abandoning the themes of middle-American life that are the strength of his poetry. Here is a selection from "Son of Babbitt," from *Against Paradise:*

> Let's nab this corner table, where you and I
> can chart the software on that girl. From here
> we can study it without embarrassing her.
> The thing in the black blouse, sipping Chablis.
> Now that's what I'd call "high" technology!
> "Is this the great, twin-meloned blouse that launched
> a thousand ships? The blouse that now, for lunch,
> chews lobster-bisque?" You smile. I understand.

The *presumption* of a businessman like me
pretending to culture, like the bourgeoisie!
Especially an executive whose name
enjoys, shall we say, such "unfortunate" fame?
Like Dickens' "Scrooge." But it's a name, my friend,
of which, I fear, I'll never hear the end.
You've surely read the book about Granddad.
You're a poet. Suppose your name were "Yeats?"
"Jon Yeats!" Well, you'd certainly debate
with yourself doing what I finally had
to do in November nineteen sixty.
I changed my name to something more discreet. (20)

The difference between Holden's earlier and more recent poetry is evident in these lines. "Son of Babbitt" is a dramatic monologue, spoken by the grandson of the infamous tycoon George Babbitt. Raised by his grandfather after his father committed suicide (crushed by the elder Babbitt's expectations), the youngest Babbitt is so ashamed of his family legacy that he changes his name. While the theme—the dark side of bourgeois life—is consistent with Holden's earliest work, the technique is not. Not only has he created a character to speak (though the character is addressing Holden), the poem is written in an irregularly rhymed iambic pentameter line, which gives a verse foundation to the poem's chatty, discursive tone. The creation of a character also gives the poem a narrative distance and irony that much of Holden's other work—usually spoken by some version of Holden himself—lacks.

In "Son of Babbitt," Holden has clearly transcended his earlier style. But what does it say when Holden himself has transcended the limits of a style he helped pioneer, and then exhaust? It does not indict that earlier period style *per se,* but it does suggest that it has reached its limit by now. When a writer and critic of Jonathan Holden's stature cannot offer any substantive reply to the Expansive poetry critique on his own terms, in his poetry or his criticism, it becomes clear how much Expansive poetry has helped to change the landscape of contemporary poetry.

If Expansive poetry's influence in the 1990s is clear, its future direction is harder to predict. As a movement—a group of like-minded poets and critics with a common purpose—it may have already done all it can do to transform the way we read and think about American poetry. What remains is the most important work of poets: writing memorable poems. As this book has demonstrated, they have already begun to do so. One can reasonably expect the same in the future. Another measure of Expansive poetry's influence is the emergence of a second generation that draws on the older poets' example. Mostly in their 30s, these poets can simply go about their work, the ground safely cleared. While it is too soon to make generalizations about these poets, one can make note of some promising first books.

Annie Finch, born in 1956, occupies a middle ground between the older and younger generations. Her critical work (discussed at length in Chapter II) has been highly influential, but her first book of poetry, *Eve,* did not appear until 1997. Finch writes with a graceful lyricism that shows there is no contradiction between feminism and form. "Coy Mistress," for instance, is a witty reply to Andrew Marvell's "To His Coy Mistress":

> Sir, I am not a bird of prey:
> a Lady does not seize the day.
> I trust that brief Time will unfold
> our youth, before he makes us old.
> How could we two write lines of rhyme
> were we not fond of numbered Time
> and grateful to the vast and sweet
> trials his days will make us meet?
> The Grave's not just the body's curse!
> No skeleton can pen a verse!
> So while this numbered World we see,
> let's sweeten Time with poetry,
> and Time, in turn, may sweeten Love
> and give us time our love to prove.
> You've praised my eyes, forehead, breast;
> you've all our lives to praise the rest. (41)

Finch's coy mistress addresses her lover by demanding time to deepen their relationship—the one thing the lover declares they do not have. The poem's smooth tetrameter couplets make the argument with wit and flair.

Born in 1967, Rachel Wetzsteon is perhaps the most precocious of the second generation of Expansive poets. *The Other Stars* (1994), her first book, was selected by John Hollander for the National Poetry Series and published by Penguin—when she was still in graduate school. *The Other Stars* is an accomplished book. Wetzsteon's style is brassy and witty; her poems move at a furious pace, at times in meter and at times in free verse, usually with regular stanzas. The collection's title poem, a sequence of unrhymed and unmetered sonnets, is a good example. Here is Section XXIV:

> The more love grows, the bigger its sealed-off
> palace becomes, and the more pinched and dark its
> stoical keeper. Inside, sun breeds space: a ray
> that snuck past the keeper enters a room and lights it—
> only now there is not one room but many.
> Beams bright as lasers but gentler give away
> the safe behind the painting, the corridor under the rug.
>
> If only the keeper, hardened by circumstance,
> could learn from this endless illumination
> and turn the room inside out. Light would then
> seep through leathery skin, giving its secrets away
> in a gradually spreading glow, turning skin the orange
> of pure beatitude. But there are only two options for the keeper:
> to be charbroiled all at once or eternally silent. (58)

Musing about her lover's absence, the speaker uses a witty image—the keeper of love locked in a palace—to explore the emotions of waiting and longing. Her conclusion, that one may be consumed or embittered by love, captures the ambivalence that often accompanies love. The poem's use of enjambment gives it force, while the two-stanza structure—seven lines each, a useful revision of traditional sonnet structure—allows it to explore both sides of its argument.

Finally, Greg Williamson's first book, *The Silent Partner*, appeared in 1995. Williamson, born in 1964, writes with a formal elegance that works equally well with lyric, dramatic, and narrative poems. "Neighboring Storms" sketches a brief narrative with lyric economy in its rhymed pentameter quatrains:

> Dark clouds are gathering. The trick knee aches.
> The hackles itch. She's breezed in drunk again,
> Precipitating fears of other men.
> Doors slam. A thunderclap of dishes shakes
>
> The wall. And when the storm outside surmounts
> Their rain of insults and their muffled threats,
> The downpour eavesdrops on their epithets,
> The wind delivers blow by blow accounts—
>
> Until it all blows over and sachets
> Of honeysuckle scent the morning air.
> They chirp like birds, and all is peaceful there.
> But me? I'm rattled. I scan the sky for days. (65)

Though a short poem, "Neighboring Storms" deeply develops its central metaphor—the calamities of natural and human weather. Of the emerging poets of the second Expansive generation, none writes with more finesse than Williamson.

These three poets, and others of their generation, are not fighting simply to establish the contemporary legitimacy of work in forms or narrative. And that is another measure—perhaps the strongest measure—of the influence of the Expansive poetry school. Narrative and formal poetry can now be judged on its merit, without the very nature of its enterprise being called into question. If for no other reason, that has earned the Expansive poets a well-defined place in American literary history. And the poems they write will earn them a larger place.

Bibliography

Allen, Dick, ed. "Expansionist Poetry: A Special Issue." *Crosscurrents* 8.2 (1988).

———. "Transcending the Self." In Allen, "Expansionist Poetry." 5–10.

Bawer, Bruce. *Prophets and Professors: Essays on the Lives and Works of Modern Poets.* Brownsville: Story Line P, 1995.

Bottoms, David, and Dave Smith, eds. *Morrow Anthology of Younger American Poets.* New York: Quill, 1985.

Byers, Thomas B. "The Closing of the American Line: Expansive Poetry and Ideology." *Contemporary Literature* 33.2 (Summer 1992): 396–415.

Conte, Joseph M. *Unending Design: The Forms of Postmodern Poetry.* Ithaca: Cornell UP, 1991.

Dacey, Philip and David Jauss. *Strong Measures: Contemporary American Poetry in Traditional Forms.* New York: Harper and Row, 1986.

Dawson, Ariel. "The Yuppie Poet." *AWP Newsletter* (May 1985).

Disch, Thomas M. *The Castle of Indolence: On Poetry, Poets and Poetasters.* New York: Picador, 1995.

———. *Dark Verses and Light.* Baltimore: Johns Hopkins UP, 1991.

———. *Yes, Let's: New and Selected Poems.* Baltimore: Johns Hopkins UP, 1989.

Dodd, Wayne. *Toward the End of the Century: Essays into Poetry.* Iowa City: University of Iowa Press, 1992.

Dooley, David. "The Contemporary Workshop Aesthetic." *Hudson Review* 43.2 (Summer 1990): 259–280.

Dove, Rita. *Thomas and Beulah.* Pittsburgh: Carnegie-Mellon UP, 1986.

Easthope, Antony. *Poetry as Discourse.* London: Methuen, 1983.

Epstein, Joseph. "Who Killed Poetry?" *Commentary* 86.2 (August 1988): 13–20.

Feirstein, Frederick. *City Life.* Brownsville: Story Line P, 1991.

——. *Ending the Twentieth Century.* Princeton: Quarterly Review of Literature, 1995.

——, ed. *Expansive Poetry: Essays on the New Narrative and New Formalism.* Santa Cruz: Story Line P, 1989.

——. *Family History.* Princeton: Quarterly Review of Literature, 1986.

——. *Fathering.* Cambridge: Apple-Wood Books, 1982.

——. *Manhattan Carnival.* Woodstock, Vermont: Countryman P, 1981.

——. *New and Selected Poems.* Brownsville: Story Line P, 1998.

——. *Survivors.* New York: Seagull Publications, 1975.

—— with Frederick Turner. Introduction to Feirstein, *Expansive Poetry.* vii–xv.

Finch, Annie. *Eve.* Brownsville, Oregon: Story Line P, 1997.

——, ed. *A Formal Feeling Comes: Poems in Form by Contemporary Women.* Brownsville, Oregon: Story Line P, 1994.

——. *The Ghost of Meter: Culture and Prosody in American Free Verse.* Ann Arbor: U of Michigan P, 1993.

——. "In Defense of Meter." *Hellas* 1.1 (1990): 21–25.

Gioia, Dana. *Can Poetry Matter? Essays on Poetry and American Culture.* St. Paul: Graywolf P, 1992.

——. "The Cult of Weldon Kees." *AWP Chronicle* 28.3 (December 1995): 1–10.

——. *Daily Horoscope.* St. Paul: Graywolf P, 1986.

——. Introduction to McDowell, *The Diviners.* ix–xii.

——. "Longfellow in the Aftermath of Modernism." *Columbia History of American Poetry.* Ed. Jay Parini. New York: Columbia UP, 1993.

——. "Meeting Mr. Cheever." *The Hudson Review* 39.3 (Autumn 1986): 419–434.

——. "Notes on the New Formalism." In Feirstein, *Expansive Poetry.* 158–175.

——. "The Poet in an Age of Prose." In McPhillips, "The New Formalism in American Poetry." 9–15.

Griffin, David Ray. *God and Religion in the Postmodern World: Essays in Postmodern Theology.* Albany: SUNY P, 1989.

Grosholz, Emily. "Art and Science." In Finch, *A Formal Feeling Comes.* 81–83.

———. *Eden.* Baltimore: Johns Hopkins UP, 1992.

———. *The River Painter.* Urbana: U of Illinois P, 1984.

———. *Shores and Headlands.* Princeton: Princeton UP, 1988.

Gross, Harvey and Robert McDowell. *Sound and Form in Modern Poetry.* Rev. ed. Ann Arbor: U of Michigan P, 1996.

Gwynn, R.S. *The Area Code of God.* West Chester: Aralia P, 1993.

———. *Bearing and Distance.* New Braunfels, Texas: Cedar Rock P, 1977.

———. *Body Bags.* In *Texas Poets in Concert: A Quartet.* Denton, Texas: U of North Texas P, 1990.

———. *The Drive–In.* Columbia: U of Missouri P, 1986.

———. *The Narcissiad.* New Braunfels, Texas: Cedar Rock P, 1981.

———. *No Word of Farewell.* West Chester: Pikeman P, 1996.

Hadas, Rachel. *The Empty Bed.* Hanover, New Hampshire: Wesleyan UP/UP of New England, 1995.

———. *Living in Time.* Newark: Rutgers UP, 1991.

———. *Mirrors of Astonishment.* Newark: Rutgers UP, 1992.

———. *Pass It On.* Princeton: Princeton UP, 1989.

———. *Slow Transparency.* Middletown, Connecticut: Wesleyan UP, 1983.

———. *A Son from Sleep.* Middletown, Connecticut: Wesleyan UP, 1987.

———. *Starting from Troy.* Boston: Godine, 1975.

Haines, John. *Fables and Distances: New and Selected Essays.* St. Paul: Graywolf P, 1996.

———. *New Poems: 1980–1988.* Brownsville: Story Line P, 1990.

Harnett, Gerald. "The New Classicism." *Hellas* 1.1 (1990): 3–8.

Hartley, George. *Textual Politics and the Language Poets.* Bloomington: Indiana UP, 1989.

Hass, Robert. *Praise.* New York: Ecco P, 1979.

Holden, Jonathan. *Against Paradise.* Salt Lake City: U of Utah P, 1990.

———. *American Gothic.* Athens: U of Georgia P, 1992.

———. *Design for a House.* Columbia: U of Missouri P, 1972.

———. *The Fate of American Poetry.* Athens: U of Georgia P, 1991.

———. *Leverage.* Charlottesville: UP of Virginia, 1982.

———. *Style and Authenticity in Postmodern Poetry.* Columbia: U of Missouri P, 1986.

———. *The Sublime.* Denton: U of North Texas P, 1996.

Jameson, Frederic. *Postmodernism, or, The Cultural Logic of Late Capitalism.* Durham: Duke UP, 1991.

Jarman, Mark. *The Black Riviera.* Middletown: Wesleyan UP, 1989.

———. *Far and Away.* Pittsburgh: Carnegie-Mellon UP, 1985.

———. *Iris.* Brownsville: Story Line P, 1992.

———. *North Sea.* Cleveland: Cleveland State University Poetry Center, 1978.

———. "Robinson, Frost and Jeffers and the New Narrative Poetry." In Feirstein, *Expansive Poetry.* 85–99.

———. *The Rote Walker.* Pittsburgh: Carnegie-Mellon UP, 1981.

——— and David Mason, eds. *Rebel Angels: Twenty-Five Poets of the New Formalism.* Brownsville: Story Line P, 1996.

——— and Robert McDowell. *The Reaper Essays.* Brownsville: Story Line P, 1996.

Jeffers, Robinson. *Rock and Hawk: A Selection of Shorter Poems.* Ed. Robert Hass. New York: Random House, 1987.

Kinzie, Mary. *The Judge is Fury: Dislocation and Form in Poetry.* Ann Arbor: U of Michigan P, 1994.

Kuzma, Greg. "Dana Gioia and the Poetry of Money." *Northwest Review* 23.3 (November 1988): 111–121.

Lake, Paul. "Toward a Liberal Poetics." In Feirstein, *Expansive Poetry.* 112–123.

Link, Franz. "The New Formalism." *Anglistic: Mitteilungen des Verbandes Deutscher Anglisten* (September 1997): 81–94.

Martin, Charles. *Room for Error.* Athens: U of Georgia P, 1978.

———. *Steal the Bacon.* Baltimore: Johns Hopkins UP, 1987.

———. *What the Darkness Proposes.* Baltimore: Johns Hopkins UP, 1996.

Mason, David. *The Buried Houses.* Brownsville, Oregon: Story Line P, 1991.

———. *The Country I Remember.* Brownsville, Oregon: Story Line P, 1996.

———. "Other Lives: On Shorter Narrative Poems." In McPhillips, "The New Formalism in American Poetry." 16–21.

McDowell, Robert. *The Diviners.* Cornwall (U.K.): Peterloo Poets, 1995.

———. "The New Narrative Poetry." In Feirstein, *Expansive Poetry.* 100–110.

———. "The Pact." West Chester: Aralia P, 1994.

————, ed. *Poetry After Modernism*. Brownsville, Oregon: Story Line P, 1991.

————. *Quiet Money*. New York: Henry Holt, 1987.

McPhillips, Robert, ed. "The New Formalism in American Poetry." *Verse* 7.3 (Winter 1990).

————. "The New Formalism and the Revival of the Love Lyric." In McPhillips, "The New Formalism in American Poetry." 22–27.

————. "Reading the New Formalists." In McDowell, *Poetry After Modernism*. 300–328.

————. "What's New About the New Formalism?" In Feirstein, *Expansive Poetry*. 195–208.

Nelson (Waniek), Marilyn. *For the Body*. Baton Rouge: Louisiana State UP, 1978.

————. *The Fields of Praise*. Baton Rouge: Louisiana State UP, 1997.

————. *The Homeplace*. Baton Rouge: Louisiana State UP, 1990.

————. *Magnificat*. Baton Rouge: Louisiana State UP, 1994.

————. *Mama's Promises*. Baton Rouge: Louisiana State UP, 1985.

————. "Sense of Discovery." In Finch, *A Formal Feeling Comes*. 241.

Newman, Wade. "Crossing the Boundary: The Expansive Movement in Contemporary Poetry." In Allen, *Expansive Poetry*. 142–153.

Ostriker, Alicia. *Stealing the Language: the Emergence of Women's Poetry in America*. Boston: Beacon P, 1986.

Peacock, Molly. *And Live Apart*. Columbia: U of Missouri P, 1980.

————. "One Green, One Blue: One Point About Formal Verse Writing and Another About Women Writing Formal Verse." In Finch, *A Formal Feeling Comes*. 175–182.

————. *Original Love*. New York: Norton, 1995.

————. *Raw Heaven*. New York: Vintage P, 1984.

————. *Take Heart*. New York: Random House, 1989.

Perelman, Bob. *The Marginalization of Poetry: Language Writing and Literary History*. Princeton: Princeton UP, 1996.

Rasula, Jed. *The American Poetry Wax Museum: Reality Effects, 1940–1990*. Urbana: NCTE, 1996.

Reinfeld, Linda. *Language Poetry: Writing as Rescue*. Baton Rouge: Louisiana State UP, 1992.

Sadoff, Ira. "Neo-Formalism: A Dangerous Nostalgia." *American Poetry Review* 18.1 (January–February 1990): 7–13.

Salter, Mary Jo. "A Beautiful Surface." In Finch, *A Formal Feeling Comes.* 190.

———. *Henry Purcell in Japan.* New York: Knopf, 1985.

———. *Unfinished Painting.* New York: Knopf, 1989.

———. *Sunday Skaters.* New York: Knopf, 1994.

Seth, Vikram. *The Golden Gate.* New York: Random House, 1986.

Shapiro, Alan. "The New Formalism." *Critical Inquiry* 14 (Autumn 1987): 200–213.

Shetley, Vernon. *After the Death of Poetry: Poet and Audience in Contemporary America.* Durham: Duke UP, 1993.

Smith, Dave and David Bottoms, eds. *The Morrow Anthology of Younger American Poets.* New York: Quill, 1985.

Spaar, Lisa Russ. Introduction to *Texas Poets in Concert: A Quartet.* Denton: U of North Texas P, 1990. 1–3.

Steele, Timothy. *The Color Wheel.* Baltimore: Johns Hopkins UP, 1994.

———. *Missing Measures: Modern Poetry and the Revolt Against Meter.* Fayetteville: U of Arkansas P, 1990.

———. *Sapphics and Uncertainties: Poems 1970–1986.* Fayetteville: U of Arkansas P, 1995.

Turner, Frederick. *April Wind and Other Poems.* Charlottesville: UP of Virginia, 1991.

———. *Beauty: the Value of Values.* Charlottesville: UP of Virginia, 1991.

———. *The Culture of Hope: A New Birth of the Classical Spirit.* New York: Free P, 1995.

———. *Genesis.* Dallas: Saybrook Publishers, 1988.

———. *Rebirth of Value: Meditations on Beauty, Ecology, Religion and Education.* Albany: SUNY P, 1991.

———. *The New World: An Epic Poem.* Princeton: Princeton UP, 1985.

———. *Tempest, Flute and Oz: Essays on the Future.* New York: Persea Books, 1991.

——— and Ernst Poppel. "The Neural Lyre." In Feirstein, *Expansive Poetry.* 209–254.

Vendler, Helen. *Soul Says: On Recent Poetry.* Cambridge: Belknap/Harvard UP, 1995.

Wakoski, Diane. "The New Conservatism in American Poetry." *American Book Review* (May–June 1986).

Walsh, William F. "Loose Talk and Literary History: Language Poetry,

New Formalism and the Construction of Taste in Contemporary American Poetry." Diss. Miami U., 1994.

Walzer, Kevin. "An Interview with Molly Peacock." *AWP Chronicle* 29.2 (October–November 1996): 1–6.

———. "An Interview with Timothy Steele." *Edge City Review* 6 (1996): 3–7.

———. "Michael J. Bugeja and Expansive Poetry's Potential." *The Hollins Critic* 33.3 (June 1996): 1–14.

———. "Natural Classicism and Constructive Postmodernism." *The Tennessee Quarterly* 2.2 (Fall 1995): 13–28.

Wetzsteon, Rachel. *The Other Stars.* New York: Penguin, 1994.

Williamson, Greg. *The Silent Partner.* Brownsville: Story Line P, 1995.

Wojahn, David. "'Yes, But': Some Thoughts on the New Formalism." *Crazyhorse* (Spring 1987).

Index